SECOND EDITION

GENDER
in the Workplace

*To my aspiring professional daughters,
Meghan and Michelle—with hopes for their "balancing
acts" and for easing of the conflicts faced at work.*

SECOND EDITION

GENDER
in the Workplace
A Case Study Approach

Jacqueline DeLaat
Marietta College

SAGE Publications
Thousand Oaks ∎ London ∎ New Delhi

For information:

 Sage Publications, Inc.
2455 Teller Road
Thousand Oaks, California 91320
E-mail: order@sagepub.com

Sage Publications Ltd.
1 Oliver's Yard
55 City Road
London EC1Y 1SP
United Kingdom

Sage Publications India Pvt. Ltd.
B-42, Panchsheel Enclave
Post Box 4109
New Delhi 110 017 India

Printed in the United States of America

Library of Congress Cataloging-in-Publication Data

DeLaat, Jacqueline.
Gender in the workplace: A case study approach/Jacqueline DeLaat, Marietta College. — 2nd ed.
    p. cm.
Includes bibliographical references.
    ISBN-13: 978-1-4129-2817-5 (pbk. : alk. paper) 1. Sex discrimination in employment—United States—Case studies. 2. Sex role in the work environment—United States—Case studies. I. College, Marietta. II. Title.

HD6060.5.U5D45 2007
306.3'6150973—dc22   2006025887

This book is printed on acid-free paper.

  07 08 09 10 11 9 8 7 6 5 4 3 2

Acquisitions Editor:	Al Bruckner
Editorial Assistant:	MaryAnn Vail
Production Editor:	Diane S. Foster
Copy Editor:	Geoffrey T. Garvey
Typesetter:	C&M Digitals (P) Ltd.
Proofreader:	Andrea Martin
Cover Designer:	Edgar Abarca

Contents

Preface

Attention to gender issues in the workplace heightened in the 1990s and has continued unabated in the new century, as men and women confront new challenges and difficulties in achieving gender equity and fair treatment at work. While sexual harassment has dominated recent public interest, other issues are also critical, such as the "glass ceiling" in advancement, sex stereotyping of certain categories of work, continual pay inequities between men and women, career development issues, and, perhaps most important, problems in balancing family needs with the structure and demands of the contemporary workplace. While most Americans accept the fairness of equal treatment for the genders in the workplace, few would argue that it has been achieved. At recent international gatherings, it has become apparent that the issues faced are worldwide, though their forms vary cross-culturally. Further, the issues appear quite complex and intransigent, despite a number of public policies directed at workplace equality both in the United States and abroad.

The purpose of the cases in this text is to raise awareness of the current forms that gender issues in the workplace are taking and to encourage active thinking about how these issues may be addressed on the personal, organizational, and public policy levels. Everyone who works or will soon work, male or female, can benefit from the exercise. While the majority of the issues are still faced far more often by women than by men, men do nonetheless encounter gender issues as well; further, men are often in a good position to affect them. Several of the cases in this collection involve men in very key roles and also introduce some ways in which they suffer from gender stereotypes and discrimination. The material should prove useful to students in a variety of college courses related to management, business, public administration, personnel management, public policy, and gender studies, and also to a wide variety of people already confronting the issues in the workforce.

❖ ACKNOWLEDGMENTS

The author wishes to thank the Faculty Development Committee and the Provost of Marietta College, Dr. Sue DeWine, for critical support at several key points in the development of these cases and for numerous international opportunities to expand their scope. I am grateful as well to the Legal Education Fund of the American Bar Association for a supportive grant during the development of the first edition in the summer of 1997. The many professional women who have shared their stories also deserve credit for being the real "teachers" involved in this project, as do my students, who have provided valuable feedback over recent years. Finally, editor Al Bruckner has provided insight for the changes in the second edition.

Introduction

Faith Daniels, the NBC news correspondent, tells an interesting story about her first "real" job after college graduation. Having been treated fairly in every way as an undergraduate mass media major, she was an honors student, mentored by a very experienced faculty member, completed a prize internship in television, and entered the job market confidently. She interviewed for a news opening with a local television station and excitedly waited for the phone call to tell her she was hired. When the call came, however, the manager said, "Well, we're sorry but we don't think you would work out in news; however, we do have an opening for a 'weather bunny' and we think you'd be great at that!" "This was my first introduction to stereotyping of women at work," Ms. Daniels later told a group of undergraduate women, "and it shows the kind of attitudes and behaviors you may run into."

Many successful working women have similar tales to tell. Younger people, however, seem to believe that gender discrimination and its causes are things of the past. While it is true that much progress toward work equity has been made in recent decades, there is substantial evidence that serious gender issues arise in many contemporary places of work around the world. This brief collection of cases is designed to help students and employees to understand what some of these issues are and to confront them in the "real life" situations presented in the case studies. Gender issues in the workplace are often subtle; they are often difficult to address, and it is often difficult to prepare students and workers to address them. Yet many can expect to be confronted with gender discrimination in the course of their careers.

Most college undergraduates, male and female, believe that gender inequality has been "solved" through public policy—legislation and court decisions—but are quite unaware of what current law actually addresses, what practices in the workplace it prohibits, and how the legal system adjudicates issues of gender and work. In addition, individual organizations and professions present unique variations of these gender issues; this is why the cases here are set in a wide variety of organizations and in several countries, though many of the lessons are easily transferable among settings.

Like Ms. Daniels, many young professionals seem totally unprepared for the gender issues they encounter. It is quite difficult for employees with very little work experience to develop individual strategies for coping with gender issues at work, should they be required to do so. Fuller understanding of these matters will greatly assist young professionals as they enter the workforce; such insights are also sought in many organizations and professional groups, through employee and management training programs addressing gender issues. This text presents a brief overview of gender issues in the workplace, along with one representative case study in the United States for each category of gender issues. The text's format and content are suitable for both undergraduate students and organizational development training in work settings.

The settings of the cases also deserve some attention. This edition includes two new cases in international settings, one in Germany and one in China. These will be useful on two counts, first showing the commonality of many of the issues worldwide, and second, showing the impact of different cultures and public policies on the forms the issues may take. The international examples are valuable to U.S. students because many of them will either work abroad, supervise workers from other cultures, or both, during their careers. The cases are set in a wide variety of organizations and professions: business, law, medicine, academia, the U.S. military, the Chinese diplomatic corps. As with the international cases, looking at the ways in which various professional settings influence the same issues is very valuable. For one consideration, we know workers will work in many organizational settings during their careers. Second, any strategies for addressing gender issues need to be specific to the organization and the culture in order to succeed. Finally, several of the cases introduce ways in which men as well as women may suffer from gender discrimination, though the vast majority of such discrimination still affects women.

❖ TOPICS

The text begins with a brief exploration of the range and types of gender issues in the workplace, organized into five categories:

1. *gender stereotypes about work* (e.g., "women don't do lumber")

2. *gender discrimination in compensation, promotion, and benefits*, e.g., the "glass ceiling"

3. *career development and mentoring*

4. *balancing work and family responsibilities*, e.g., child care, dual-career couples, pregnancy issues

5. *sexual harassment issues*

Later in this introduction, I will define these five categories of issues and provide concrete examples of the issues in each category, chosen from a variety of current work environments. Relevant data and research on the issues will also be summarized, along with key definitions, and some illustrative examples and concepts. (The intent, however, is to provide a broad overview of these issues, useful in a variety of teaching settings, rather than an in-depth, specialized summary of the research, which is readily available elsewhere.) This material will familiarize students or trainees with the broad range of gender issues in the workplace and help bring order to the material by grouping issues in useful categories.

Each of the seven chapters is a case study illustrating one particular category of gender issues. For example, Chapter 1 presents the case Half a Pie, or None? that focuses upon gender stereotyping of certain positions within an organization. The cases are all based upon real situations; several were drawn from federal court cases, while others were developed from in-depth personal interviews. The two international cases focus respectively on sex stereotyping of work and work and family balance; each follows the case representing this same issue in the United States. The Student Responses promote analysis and evaluation of information in the case, as well as presenting activities that may enhance learning from the case. (Instructor's Notes, providing additional background information useful in discussing the issues, are contained in an important companion volume.)

I emphasize case studies here as an innovative teaching technique, well suited to the objectives of increasing awareness of how actual workers, both men and women, as well as the law and the legal system, address gender issues in the workplace. Both students and employees may have very little experience with gender issues, and the use of case studies provides an effective way of increasing their ability to apply what they learn. Without concrete application, the study of gender issues can seem remote indeed, especially to undergraduates. Traditional treatment of gender issues focuses upon both the theory of gender and data or evidence that gender discrimination occurs. While this work is very valuable, it tends to be rather theoretical. The use of some specific case studies, which engage learners more actively and directly in the issues, makes the gender content of many undergraduate and graduate courses, as well as training on gender within work organizations, much more concrete. Case studies can thus extend the experience and perspective of both students and employees who might not have encountered certain issues personally.

The case studies included in the book are based on actual legal cases, nationally reported incidents, or personal interviews, but the names of all people and places and dialogue are fictitious.

The development of cases involves researching the legal issues, choosing a good illustrative case, writing the case in a story or scenario format, and developing key objectives and questions for analysis. In some case studies, classroom simulations may be used to recreate the circumstances presented in the case and allow student responses. In all cases, discussion questions focused on the critical events in the case encourage the students to think about the gender, legal, and managerial issues in a concrete situation, thus greatly enhancing classroom or training site discussion and participation. Case studies place students directly "in the action," by requiring problem solving and personally developed responses to the situations presented. For example, in a case about gender stereotyping of work, both supervisors and the individual being denied access to certain work have practical and legal options and responsibilities; the case includes activities that reflect both these perspectives on the work situation. Case studies thus help to promote lively, active learning environments, in which most people can learn more readily than in a more passive environment.

The Conclusion is devoted to an examination of the connections between the five categories of gender issues explored in the cases. For example, sexual stereotyping of work often leads to inequities in compensation or promotion. The Conclusion highlights the importance of the organizational culture and how to change its treatment of gender issues. Students or trainees who complete all seven cases will be able to compare the differences between organizations and cultures that affect both the nature of a gender issue and how it might be most effectively addressed. Solutions that are feasible in an academic environment, for example, may not be effective in the military because of differences in the nature, values, and mission or goals of the organizations. And, obviously, what works in the United States may not work at all in China. Consider, next, a brief introduction to each of the five categories of gender issues in the workplace.

❖ GENDER STEREOTYPING OF WORK

Regarding certain types or categories of work as male and others as female constitutes gender stereotyping of work. Industrial sociologists, among others, have studied such patterns in the U.S. workforce over time, and U.S. Census data about the gender composition of various professions and jobs provide the data for such analyses. During the 1970s and 1980s, occupational sex segregation declined for the first time in the twentieth century (Reskin & Padavic, 2002, p. 73). A variety of social and legal, as well as economic, factors contributed to this decline, including passage and initial enforcement of Title VII of the 1964 Civil Rights Act, the emergence of the second women's movement of the century in the 1970s, and an increase in educational opportunities for women resulting from other federal policies such as Title IX of the Education Amendments of 1972, which requires all educational institutions receiving federal money to treat men and women equally. As of the turn of the century, the sex segregation index for jobs held stood at 52, compared to 62 in 1980 (Reskin & Padavic, 2002, p. 74). (In a perfectly integrated organization the index would be 0.) The numbers of women in many formerly male professions—notably law, medicine, government, and academia—have increased dramatically in this period. One of the most important contributing factors has been the greater similarity in the percentages of men and women graduating from college, in their college majors, and in their choices of postgraduate education. In 1960 38% of all college graduates were female, but the percentage has risen steadily since then and passed the 50% mark in the early 1980s. Only 3% of all professional degrees were granted to women in 1960, but by 1987 that percentage was 35% (Goldin, 1990). Half of current law school graduates are female (Catalyst, 2005b), and women have also caught up with men in medical education (Jacobs & Berkowitz, 2002). Special efforts to attract women to engineering and the sciences are also bearing fruit (National Council for Research on Women, 2001). Women and men are now equally likely to hold jobs in the management category of jobs (Powell & Graves, 2003).

It is also clear that sex segregation persists in the workforce. The stark occupational data confirm that women and men are still segregated into distinct careers, despite the reduction in the overall amount of such segregation in the past few decades. The ten most common occupations for women, according to 2000 census data, were (in order): secretary; manager/administrator; cashier; supervisor or proprietor, salesperson; registered nurse; teacher, elementary; nurse's aide, orderly, attendant; bookkeeper; waitress; receptionist. For men, the list is as follows: salaried manager, administrator; supervisor or proprietor, salesperson; truck driver; janitor; carpenter; cook; computer systems analyst and scientist; sales representative; mining, manufacturing, and wholesale laborer, except construction; supervisor, production occupations (Reskin & Padavic, 2002, p. 66, calculated from 1998, 1999, and 2000 U.S. Current Population Survey data). It is also clear that the occupations dominated by women are less compensated and less valued than those dominated by men (U.S. Bureau of Labor Statistics, 2004a). The gain in women in management masks, as Powell and Graves note, the persistent low numbers of women in top management positions; this helps explain the 67/100 female/male pay ratio among managers (Powell & Graves, 2003, p. 30).

As Reskin and Padavic so ably summarize, this segregation persists because of a variety of factors: the actions of employers, actions of male workers and actions of female workers, sex labeling of jobs, recruitment practices, and outdated assumptions all contribute to occupational segregation by gender (2002, pp. 74–95). While, as Goldin (1990) reports, most explicit rules prohibiting women from certain types of work, or requiring them to resign upon marriage, are now illegal, the impact of these earlier practices remains. It is also correct that if women's work has been characterized in one way, and men's work in another, few individuals may be willing to oppose that established pattern (p. 8).

These social norms help perpetuate job segregation, even though it is illegal. Employers may discriminate intentionally or unintentionally, both of which, of course, violate Title VII. Recruitment practices, interviewing questions and techniques, and stereotypes of initial recruiters or gatekeepers can all operate to discriminate unfairly against one gender. Further, requirements or skill qualifications may be unfair and operate against women or men; at times one sex is provided with better training opportunities denied to the other, which is also an unfair practice. Employers' control of workplace rules and structure (such as location and hours of work or shift rotations) may also operate to discourage women or men from entering a certain type of work or from advancement.

In addition to employers' actions, one gender of coworkers may create an atmosphere or workplace dynamic that effectively excludes the other. For example, men often fear the entry of women into their profession for a variety of reasons, including the new competition, a decline in the prestige of the work, the need to clean up workplace behavior or language, or the fear that women may not do their share (Reskin & Padavic, 2002, pp. 91–93). Some men thus feel they have a stake in keeping women out of their work and act on this feeling. Of course some of these actions may be illegal.

Women, themselves, may contribute to their occupational segregation. To the extent that women do not pursue careers they obviously cannot develop them. While choices of men and women may "voluntarily" exclude them from a certain type of work, Reskin and Padavic's (2002) analysis—that such "free choice" is largely socially and organizationally determined—is compelling (p. 79). Recent work argues that in the current era it is not clear that women avoid seeking the same careers and the same job satisfactions that men do; the numbers of women in the permanent workforce, and research about them, indicate the changes from previous eras in this regard (Jacobs & Gerson, 2004; Jacobs & Madden, 2004). It is more likely that women modify their career objectives and choices because of a combination of socialization, role-conflict, and organizational and professional realities than from true free choice.

In the case Half a Pie, or None issues of occupational segregation by gender are raised in the context of a highly trained, professional woman seeking career advancement to managerial levels. The case illustrates ways in which employer actions can lead to occupational segregation, in spite of the legal ban on such actions provided in Title VII. The actions of supervisors as well as coworkers, both male and female, are important in the case.

In One Step Forward, Two Steps Back? gender stereotyping of work is much more blatant, in that several career options for women are matters of public policy in China.

❖ GENDER DISCRIMINATION IN
  COMPENSATION, PROMOTION, AND BENEFITS

A second area of gender discrimination in the workforce is compensation and advancement. Government and private research has authoritatively documented the pay gap in earnings between men and women; in 1992 women earned about 74 cents for each dollar earned by men (Karsten, 1994, p. 53); in 2002 the figure was 76 cents on the dollar (U.S. Bureau of Labor Statistics, 2002, in Powell & Graves, 2003, p. 35).

Part of the gap, of course, is related to the occupational segregation of women, and the corresponding lower pay rates for "women's jobs." The improvement in women's salaries has been in part due to their entrance into formerly all-male professions.

But there is also much discrepancy between the earnings of men and women even *within the same* occupation. Only about 7% of the gap, within certain occupations, can be accounted for by education and experience differences between men and women. In fact, the female/male (F/M) salary ratio for full-time workers in some highly educated and prestigious professions is as follows: 68% for physicians; 67% for managers; 75% for college and university professors; 69% for lawyers; 88% for registered nurses. Thus, "the depressing fact for women is that the higher the educational attainment, the *lower* the F/M ratio, a depressing thought for females," (Powell & Graves, 2003, p. 30). This tends to discredit the pipeline theory, which has argued that women have not been "in the pipeline" long enough to gain the experience needed for top-level positions. (The larger number of women remaining in the workforce throughout their adult life also discredits the pipeline theory in the current context.)

As in cases of occupational segregation, there is significant national policy against unequal pay and related practices, in the Equal Pay Act of 1963. The act was passed as an amendment to the Fair Labor Standards Act of 1938; it stipulates that men and women must be compensated equally for jobs that are alike in content, that require similar skill, effort, and responsibility, and that are performed under similar working conditions. The act covers incentives and employee benefits as well as wages. Women and men may be paid different rates for doing the same work only on the basis of a legitimate seniority or merit system. The act applies only to pay discrimination within the same job.

The current movement toward *comparable worth* policies argues that the equal pay principle should extend to work of similar difficulty, even if the jobs, themselves, are different. Since men and women are not always found doing the exact same work in the same place, and so on, the comparable worth concept argues that equal pay should apply to *equivalent* work. The problem is determining comparability. Various methods of judging the difficulty, skill, and responsibility, among other factors, required in a job have been utilized to judge comparability. Despite its implementation by a number of state governments and private corporations, this movement is still controversial, whereas the basic equal pay policy—equal pay for the same work—is generally accepted.

Even as women enter more lucrative fields, however—such as law, medicine, engineering, business—it is apparent that their advancement to the highest and best paid levels of these professions has been limited. Currently, for example, women hold only about 13% of the upper management positions in U.S. Fortune 500 corporations; at the very top of corporations, just 6% of CEO positions were held by women in 2000 (Catalyst, 2005a). Further, the pay gap is greater at the vice president level or above; women's salaries at this level are only 58% of their male peers' salaries (U.S. Bureau of Labor Statistics, 2004a). In government, as well, their advancement to top career positions has not been nearly commensurate with their numbers; by 1998, for example, women held 45% of federal jobs but just 22% of top management positions (Reskin & Padavic, 2002, p. 103).

No definitive single explanation of the pay gap has been proposed; suggestions include organizational barriers to advancement, career interruptions, and women's desires to combine strong commitment to both work and family roles. The existence of artificial barriers to women's advancement in organizations has been termed the glass ceiling. In the Civil Rights Act of 1991 a federal glass ceiling commission was created, within the U.S. Department of Labor, to do systematic research on the extent of the glass ceiling problem, its apparent causes, and policies that might help remediate it. (Major recommendations of this commission before its expiration in 1996 are reported in Appendix B to Chapter 3.)

In summary, the commission succeeded in documenting the existence of the glass ceiling and identifying the specific formal and informal barriers of which it is composed. The commission found, for example, that top managers assess male and female workers differently. Men are evaluated on perceived potential, but women are more often judged on past accomplishments (Karsten, 1994, p. 16). Further, in related research, only 8% of 201 CEOs of America's largest business firms (most of whom were male) said that women "lacked the aggressiveness" to be top managers, and only 5% said women needed to be more willing to relocate to progress in their careers, thus somewhat debunking two common explanations for women's failure to reach the highest corporate levels (Fisher, 1992).

The case Did Attorney Evans Bump Her Head on the Glass Ceiling? deals with the judgments made about advancement or promotion of professionals—in this case, attorneys—and the complexity of these decisions. It delves into the internal operations of a law firm to examine the process for selecting full partners. Issues about both formal and informal factors that affect such decisions are relevant to the case. Students will judge whether the glass ceiling operated in this instance.

Issues of advancement and compensation are very clearly related to each of the other four categories of gender-related workplace issues represented in this text. The interaction of compensation and advancement issues with occupational segregation or stereotyping has been mentioned; in the Conclusion attention will return to this interaction, as well as the connections of compensation and advancement issues with those of career development and balancing work and family commitments.

❖ CAREER DEVELOPMENT AND MENTORING

An examination of career development grows logically out of the documentation of barriers to women's advancement. In attempting to break the glass ceiling, professions, work organizations, and individuals have turned to a more detailed look at the ways in which successful careers develop, the necessary ingredients of success in various professions and organizations, and gender differences in the opportunities for successful career development. The pipeline theory, previously mentioned, assumed that as women were present in careers for the requisite number of years they would naturally progress at rates similar to those of men in the same positions and holding the same general credentials. These, after all, are the basic tenets of equal treatment, and agreement that such opportunity is important formed the societal consensus in support of the equal treatment provisions of the civil-rights and equal-pay policies mentioned earlier. Forty-plus years after the passage of these policies, however, it is clear from the data previously cited that women are not progressing in rates similar to those of men, even when their basic qualifications and experience are similar (National Commission on Pay Equity, 1991).

It is now common, as a result, for individual professions and occupational groups to analyze the career paths of successful leaders within their fields. Women in both law and medicine, for example, have undertaken systematic research into the reasons for their lack of equality—in both positions attained and overall compensation—with men in their profession. Similarly, women in academia have begun to study the reasons for both their lower numbers and the small percentage of positions they held at the highest levels, and a wide variety of studies of women in corporate America have documented the obstacles to women seeking top positions there. This type of attention, within a variety of organizations and professions, has highlighted the importance of career planning and mentoring for the professional advancement of both men and women. But it appears that women face some special difficulties in this regard.

First, for many years women thought of their paid work in terms of jobs rather than careers. The woman in a two-earner family often considered herself, and was certainly considered by others, as the second income. Jobs were often held by women for short periods of time and were accepted or abandoned according to the immediate needs of her family and the degree of flexibility offered by her husband's employment. Of course, some women were the single earners for their families, even in earlier eras, but that was the exception rather than the rule. The previously mentioned employment trends of women in recent decades have altered this picture, however; many women are in the workforce permanently, they have higher degrees of education and experience, and they seek careers rather than jobs. Thus, they need the same career planning and career development experiences as men.

Many young women are still reluctant to commit to long-term career planning and have difficulty finding assistance in such planning within their professions and work organizations. Men who are in supervisory or senior positions are more likely to offer to mentor young men than young women. There are often few, if any, senior women in organizations that might be available to mentor younger women. Young women are uncomfortable asking for mentoring from older men—and the men may be unwilling to offer mentoring—because of the possible connotations that might be placed on such relationships. Thus, young women are at a disadvantage in seeking mentoring relationships, which the Glass Ceiling Commission and others have determined to be critical to professional advancement.

Medical Mentoring addresses these issues in the context of women developing careers in medicine. The case focuses on the recent experiences of women in medicine and reflects the personal views of a group of female physicians about these issues. Formal mentoring arises as an option in the case, and individuals discuss a number of mentoring models and difficulties with mentoring programs. Students will develop their own suggestions for mentoring in response to the case situation.

❖ BALANCING WORK AND FAMILY RESPONSIBILITIES

To all observers of modern gender roles in the United States, it is clear that the nature of families and the performance of family responsibilities have undergone dramatic change at the same time that the increases in women in the workforce have occurred. Among mothers of children under age 18, 78.1% worked by 2003 (U.S. Bureau of Labor

Statistics, 2004b). A substantial majority (62.5%) of women with children under the age of 6 years now works outside the home. In 1977 32% of mothers with children younger than 1 year were in the labor force (Goldin, 1990), but by 2003 the percentage had increased to 53.7% (Employment Policy Foundation, 2004). Further, many women are now single heads of household, charged with both child rearing and earning an income. Many families with children no longer have either parent available in the household during the day; as of 2003 66% of parents were in marriages where both parents worked (Catalyst, 2005c). Thus, many children are cared for by nonfamily members or grandparents, and many children are on their own after school. In addition, even within two-parent households, fathers and mothers are more apt to share family responsibilities that were once totally borne by the mothers.

These changes have prompted many workers—male and female—to support changes in the workplace such as flextime, job sharing, working from home or telecommuting, on-site child care, family and parental leave, and other family support measures. Recent studies indicate that, in a more competitive employment market, some progressive employers are more than willing to provide many family services as perks of employment. In 2002, however, only 10% of large companies provided on-site child care (Symonds, 2002) and as of 2004 only 14% of all workers in private industry had access to employer assistance for either providing or locating child care. The larger the number of workers, the more likely the employer was to provide such services, but the overall picture is discouraging (U.S. Bureau of Labor Statistics, 2004b). Thus, many workers must still go it alone when it comes to balancing the demands of their work and the needs of their families. Hall (1990) found that, for example, 73% of mothers and 35% of fathers report "a lot of stress" in trying to mesh work and family roles, while 11% of the women (and none of the men) encountered "extreme" stress from this source. Recent work confirms that stress between work and family remains a major problem (Jacobs & Gerson, 2004).

Further, a number of studies indicate that, in a majority of families with children in which both parents work outside the home, the mothers still feel more responsibility for child-care issues and provision than do fathers. Working from home, as well, introduces some complexity in the balancing of family and work responsibilities. In addition, household maintenance and errands appear to be, still, primarily the woman's responsibility in a majority of working families (Coltrane, 2004). According to one estimate, the total hours all women work in the workplace and in the household increased by 5% between

1959 and 1983, while those for men decreased by 9% (Goldin, 1990, p. 212). Fathers have, however, increased their time commitments in the home somewhat. In the late 1990s, coresident fathers were available to their children about three-fourths as much as the working mother, interacting on weekdays about two-thirds as often but more on weekends (Pleck & Masciadrelli, 2003). Fathers *are* assuming more family responsibilities; family concerns generally, however, still receive more time and physical and emotional attention from women than from men. In addition, the average woman still does about twice the amount of routine housework as the average man, so the persistence of gender roles in the family continues. Further, there is some indication that "changes in the elite professions (in sharing of family responsibilities) may be lagging behind change in the working class" (Coltrane, 2004).

Government policy on these matters has focused primarily on the financial burdens of paying for child care. The Family and Medical Leave Act of 1993 represents the only national public policy addressed to other family concerns of the employed; it provides for unpaid leave for a variety of family needs, and is included here as Appendix A to the Pregnant Professor case. The 1995 Welfare Reform Act continues a federal policy of providing some subsidized child care to lower-income families (it was due for reauthorization in the U.S. Congress in 2005 but was not addressed as scheduled), and tax law revisions in the 1997 Taxpayer Relief Act extended some deductions to other families for child-related expenses. The needs of their children and, increasingly, of their elderly parents as well continue to be a major concern of working women and men in all types of professions and work situations. In most families, though, women continue to carry more of this responsibility (Coltrane, 2004). Balancing the needs of families and the demands of work, then, continues to be an important gender-related issue in the workplace.

The case The Pregnant Professor raises some of these issues as they affect a dual-career couple in academia. The couple portrayed in the case takes an egalitarian approach to both family and professional issues and decisions. Issues of pregnancy-leave policies, career development in the context of high employer expectations, commuting marriage arrangements, and the stress of combining professional and young family responsibilities all emerge in this case. Students view these matters through the eyes of the couple experiencing them in the early years of their careers and marriage.

Important work documents the fact that these work-family conflicts are international in scope. Consistent with earlier international studies, a 2000 study of men and women holding high positions in politics and private business in 27 nations clearly shows that "these leaders face the dilemma of combining a demanding career and family life" and that they manage it in a variety of ways (Vianello & Moore, 2000). Social and cultural contexts as well as public policies shape the experiences of these women and men. Both the international cases in this collection also raise issues of family roles; Kinder, Kirche, Küche: Working Mothers in Germany reveals a German businesswoman's dilemmas over parenting while pursuing a demanding managerial career, and in One Step Forward, Two Steps Back, an aspiring Chinese diplomat has to consider family and marriage issues as well as formal barriers that complicate her career path. These cases also include significant differences in societal norms about families and different governmental responses to family needs.

❖ SEXUAL HARASSMENT ISSUES

The Anita Hill sexual harassment charges against Supreme Court nominee Clarence Thomas in 1991, as well as charges against the president and several other prominent leaders later in that decade, have focused attention upon issues of sexual harassment in the workplace. The development of organizational policies and procedures for dealing with sexual harassment is now commonplace, though the effectiveness of many of these policies remains to be demonstrated.

The extent of harassment appears far more widespread than many initially believed, with close to half of American working women reporting in a variety of surveys that they have encountered some form of harassment at work. Surveys conducted in the 1970s and 1980s estimated that between 57% and 88% of employees had been harassed then (Ford & McLaughlin, 1988). In 1991 53% of 1,300 members of the National Association of Female Executives reported they or someone they knew had been harassed at work (Galen, Weber, & Cuneo, 1991). The Equal Employment Opportunity Commission (EEOC) reported 13,176 complaints in 2004; 15.1% of these were filed by men, a percentage that increased steadily from 1992 on. The vast majority of claims complained of treatment by men. Examples abound. Since the turn of the century sexual harassment claims have been made by women in major financial firms, corporations, law firms, the media, the military academies, and the armed forces in Iraq. In one large national survey 47.7% of all women physicians reported having experienced gender-based harassment (defined as harassment related to being female in a traditionally male environment, without a sexual or physical component), and 36.9% reported sexual harassment (defined as harassment with a sexual or physical component) (Frank & Schiffman, 1998).

It is believed that at least one-third of women in the United States experience some form of sexual harassment. In studies of sexual harassment in American companies, psychologist Louise Fitzgerald discovered that 40 to 60% of women in these companies experienced some form of harassing behavior. These studies, based on responses to Fitzgerald's renowned Sexual Experiences Questionnaire, have been used extensively in the most important sexual harassment litigation in the United States (Murray, 1998). In addition, the U.S. government reported that 44% of women employed by the federal government had experienced harassment from 1992 to 1994 (U.S. Merit Systems Protection Board, 1995). The first task in addressing this issue appears to be that of defining the types of harassment so that the behaviors become recognizable. Beyond that initial step, training and awareness programs are needed to reduce the incidence of harassment in the workplace. Strong commitment to a policy of no tolerance on the part of top management also appears to be an essential ingredient in efforts to reduce sexual harassment.

Research suggests that most sexual harassment is committed by men against women, although the reverse is certainly possible, and same-sex harassment too has been declared illegal by the U.S. Supreme Court. Harassment is also most often an issue of power, with harassers often holding organizational power or supervisory authority over those they harass. Harassment is defined thus: "Unwelcome sexual advances, requests for sexual favors, and other verbal or physical conduct of a sexual nature constitutes sexual harassment when submission to or rejection of this conduct explicitly or implicitly affects an individual's employment, unreasonably interferes with an individual's work performance or creates an intimidating, hostile or offensive work environment" (U.S. EEOC, 2004). The two types of harassment are quid pro quo harassment, which involves the provision or denial of favorable job conditions, pay raises, or promotions on the basis of acceptance or rejection of requests for sexual favors, and hostile environment sexual harassment, which occurs when verbal, physical, or graphic sexual displays are so pervasive that they interfere with work performance or cause an offensive or intimidating atmosphere in the workplace.

Harassment is difficult to address because it usually requires the less powerful in a work organization to confront the more powerful. It is also often the case that a general atmosphere or culture in the organization exists in support of the harassing behaviors, especially those of the hostile environment variety and those involving less physical behavior. As more and more young workers devote much of their time to their careers, it is also possible that many more office romances are likely to develop. Distinguishing these mutual relationships and behaviors from the unwelcome sexual harassment activity can also be a complicated exercise in some instances. Finally, the legal definitions of sexual harassment, and who may be held accountable for it, are in flux and being developed by the courts case by case. This means that many employees and organizations are understandably unclear both about what behavior is unacceptable and about what organizations need to do to help reduce or eliminate it from the workplace.

Sexual Harassment in the Military, the sexual harassment case in this collection, is based upon actual incidents that occurred from the mid-1990s to the mid-oughts. Revealed from the perspectives of both alleged victims of the harassment and military leaders attempting to eliminate it, the case illustrates the importance of the power relationship between harassers and their victims in perpetuating the harassment behaviors. The difficulty of creating effective protections and procedures for dealing with harassment is also clear in this case. Finally, the case documents the extent of harassment in the military over a period of years and asks students to confront the issue of how to change an organizational culture that has tolerated harassment to this extent.

❖ EFFECTIVE USE OF THE TEXT

This book envisions an active classroom or learning environment, in which both students and teachers are committed to exploring these gender issues up close and personal. From the student or trainee perspective, the best way to utilize the cases is to read them in advance of the group discussions and contemplate each of the questions or assignments in the Student Response section carefully. The most effective learning will occur when students are able to truly place themselves within the case and approach assignments and discussion of the issues from the perspective of those involved in the case. If the instructor suggests, some additional reading on topics related to the cases may also be useful in developing perspective.

From the instructor or facilitator's point of view it is important to fully review the Instructor's Notes for each case, as they provide additional resources and information that will assist in the discussion of case issues. Epilogues to each case, also presented in the Instructor's Notes, reveal which course of action the actual principals in the case pursued and what occurred as a result. Some additional teaching suggestions and techniques are also offered in the Notes. Instructors should feel free, however, to adapt these suggested assignments to the particular class or training setting in which the cases are being used.

Further, instructors and facilitators should try to maintain the position that there is no right answer to the problems or assignments posed in the cases, for, in fact, that is true. If we knew the right answer to balancing work and family, preventing sexual harassment, developing women's long-term careers, eliminating the glass ceiling, and so on, there would be no need for cases to explore the dilemmas these issues pose in the contemporary workplace. Rather, we could simply teach the solutions. As this discussion indicates, however, these gender issues in the workplace are more complex and varied than a single solution or approach encompasses. Meanwhile, scholars and practitioners in a wide variety of organizations are earnestly exploring alternative ways of addressing these problems. The cases' value, then, lies in the validity and complexity of the issues they pose and their power to engage students and instructors alike in exploring possible effective actions addressing these issues. A particular student's response, then, *if well reasoned and based on the facts at hand*, is just as likely to have merit as anyone else's. Instructors who can maintain that view and a general stance of openness about the questions that the cases raise make the most effective use of the text.

❖ RELATED READINGS

Catalyst. (2005a). *Rate of women's advancement to top corporate officer positions slow, new catalyst tenth anniversary census shows.* Retrieved August 22, 2006, at: www.catalystwomen.org/files/quicktakes/Quick%20Takes%20-%20 Women%20in%20Law.pdf#search=%22Quick%20Takes%3A%20 Women%20in%20law%22

Catalyst. (2005b). *Quick takes: Women in law.* Retrieved August 22, 2006, at: www.catalystwomen.org/files/quicktakes/Quick%20Takes%20-%20Women%20in%20Law.pdf#search=%22Quick%20Takes%3A%20 Women%20in%20law%22

Catalyst. (2005c). *Quick takes: Working and stay-at-home mothers.* Retrieved August 22, 2006, at: www.catalystwomen.org/files/quicktakes/Quick%20 Takes%20-%20Working%20Mothers.pdf

Civil Rights Act of 1964, Title VII, 42 U.S.C. §701 (1981). Retrieved August 22, 2006, at: www.eeoc.gov/policy/vii.html

Cockburn, C. (1991). *In the way of women: Men's resistance to sex equality in organizations.* Ithaca: New York State School of Industrial and Labor Relations, Cornell University.

Coltrane, S. (2004, November). Elite careers and family commitment: It's (still) about gender. *Annals of the American Academy of Political and Social Science, 596,* 214–220.

Employment Policy Foundation. (2004). More mothers in the labor force this mother's day. Press release. Retrieved June 30, 2006 at: http://www .epf.org/news/release.asp?nrid=109

Epstein, C. F. (1993). *Women in law.* Urbana: University of Illinois Press.

Fisher, A. (1992, September 21). When will women get to the top? *Fortune, 126*(6), 44–56.

Ford, R., & McLaughlin, F. (1988, November/December). Sexual harassment at work. *Business Horizons, 31*(6), 14–19.

Frank, B., & Schiffman, R. (1998, February 23). Prevalence and correlates of harassment among US women physicians. *Internal Medicine, 158,* 352–358.

Galen, M., Weber, J., & Cuneo, A. (1991, October 18). Sexual harassment: Out of the shadows. *BusinessWeek, 31,* 14–19.

Goldin, C. (1990). *Understanding the gender gap: An economic history of American women.* Oxford, UK: Oxford University Press.

Hall, D. (1990, winter). Balancing work life and home life: What can organizations do to help? *Academy of Management Executive, 2,* 213–223.

Jacobs, J. A., & Berkowitz, R. (2002). Age and college completion: A life-history analysis of women aged 15–44. *Sociology of Education, 75,* 211–230.

Jacobs, J. A., & Gerson, K. (2004). *The time divide: Work, family and gender inequality.* Cambridge, MA: Harvard University Press.

Jacobs, J. A., & Madden, J. F. (Eds.). (2004, November). *Annals of the American Academy of Political and Social Science, 596.*

Karsten, M. F. (1994). *Management and gender: Issues and attitudes.* Westport, CT: Praeger.

Moen, P., & Han, S. K. (2001). Gendered careers: A life-course perspective. In R. Hertz & N. L. Marshall (Eds.), *Working families: The transformation of the American home.* (42–57). Berkeley: University of California Press.

Murray, B. (1998, August). Psychology's voice in sexual harassment law. *American Psychological Association Monitor, 21,* 58.

National Commission on Pay Equity. (1991). After 28 years, equal pay for equal work still not achieved. *Newsnotes, 12,* 3.

National Council for Research on Women. (2001). *Balancing the equation: Where women are in science, engineering, and technology.* Retrieved June 30, 2006 at: www.ncrw.org/publications/pubs.htm

Pleck, J. H., & Masciadrelli, B. P. (2003). Paternal involvement: Levels, sources and consequences. In M. E. Lam (Ed.), *The role of the father in child development* (4th ed.) (pp. 181–204). New York: John Wiley.

Powell, G. N., & Graves L. M. (2003). *Women and men in management* (3rd ed.). Thousand Oaks, CA: Sage.

Pregnancy Discrimination Act of 1978, 42 U.S.C. §701(k) (1981).

Reskin, B., & Padavic, I. (2002). *Women and men at work* (2d ed.). Thousand Oaks, CA: Sage.

Rhode, D. (2001). *The unfinished agenda: Women in the legal profession.* Chicago: American Bar Association Commission on Women in the Profession.

Symonds, W. C. (2002, June 10). The killer perk. *BusinessWeek,* p. 101. www.businessweek.com/magazine/content/02_23/b3786610.htm?chan= search

U.S. Bureau of the Census. (1990, 2000). Detailed occupation and other characteristics from the EEO File for the United States. Retrieved August 22, 2006, at: www.census.gov/eeo2000/index.html

U.S. Bureau of Labor Statistics. (2004a). *Current population survey,* Table 39, Median weekly earnings of full-time and salaried workers by detailed occupation and sex. Retrieved August 18, 2006, at: www.bls.gov/cps/cpsaaT39.pdf

U.S. Bureau of Labor Statistics. (2004b). *Employee benefits survey.* Percent of all workers with access to employer assistance for child care. Retrieved August 22, 2006, at: http://data.bls.gov/cgi-bin/surveymost

U.S. Equal Employment Opportunity Commission. (2004). Statistics, sexual harassment. Retrieved August 22, 2006, at: www.eeoc.gov/stats/harass .html

U.S. Merit Systems Protection Board. (1995). *Sexual harassment in the federal workforce: Trends, progress and continuing challenges.* Washington, DC: U.S. Government Printing Office.

Vianello, M., & Moore, M. (2000). *Gendering elites: Economic and political leadership in 27 industrialized societies.* New York: Macmillan.

Wax, A. (2004). Family-friendly workplace reform: The prospects for change. In J. A. Jacobs and J. F. Manning (Eds.), Mommies and daddies on the fast track [Special issue]. *Annals of the American Academy of Political and Social Science 596,* 36–61.

Why the gap remains a chasm. (2004, June 14). *BusinessWeek,* p. 58.

Case Studies

1

Half a Pie, or None?

❖ BODY OF CASE

"Are you prepared to accept our offer of the position of project manager, Ms. Andersen?" asked Mr. Green, president of Computing Central.

Ms. Andersen recalled her hours considering this reduced offer, which she had suspected would be forthcoming, in contrast to the position for which she had actively applied. To accept "half a pie" or not

3

posed the first of many dilemmas she would face regarding Computer Central and the next stage of her career.

Background

Kirsten Andersen was by this time a highly qualified senior management consultant and business developer. She had extensive training and experience in market and business development. Holding a B.A. in economics and international marketing, M.A. degrees in international communication and international law and organization, and a finance certificate from the Wharton School of Business, she had also completed all the course work for a doctorate in political sociology.

In the previous 5 years Ms. Andersen built a successful consulting firm that helped develop research, design, and implementation of foreign market entry strategies, and integration of technical systems for 15 Fortune 200 companies. In the previous year Ms. Andersen had sold her firm for more than 2 million dollars and pondered her next career move. Her goals were to acquire more technical consulting and business development experience abroad and to work within a major corporate structure to enhance her marketability for senior executive positions. She also wanted an opportunity to aggressively pursue the high earnings she had attained in her own firm.

The "Half a Pie" Offer

Early in her job search a colleague provided entry to Computer Central, a European firm developing new technical enterprises in the emerging democracies of Eastern Europe that was part of the worldwide umbrella corporation Techniques Advantage. Computer Central retained its most qualified personnel in the position of evaluator, who assess new projects and present recommendations to clients about technical strategy. The position also carried with it substantial sales and bonus income potential. Attaining an evaluator's slot, then, would have met all Ms. Andersen's career objectives at the time of the interview.

Ms. Andersen was interviewed for the evaluator's position at Computer Central a few months later. She met with Mr. Jones, vice president of Computer Central, as well as with Mr. Green, the firm's president. She was also interviewed by CEO Charles, worldwide head of Techniques Advantage. Each of these individuals told her in interviews that she was well qualified to be an evaluator; Mr. Green, in particular, told her that "You will be an asset to our evaluators team."

Mr. Green also told Ms. Andersen that Mr. Jones said, "She definitely is an evaluator."

Later that month Mr. Green submitted Ms. Andersen's name for final approval for appointment as an evaluator. Shortly thereafter, however, he reported to Ms. Andersen that CEO Charles of Techniques Advantage stated she could not be hired as an evaluator because "No woman will be on my evaluators team." Mr. Charles had privately elaborated his opinion that the energy, drive, and commitment required of evaluators was beyond what most women could offer a firm.

Mr. Green then attempted to persuade Ms. Andersen to come to work for Computer Central under a different job title. He assured her informally that she would be given evaluator duties and eventually converted to the proper job title once she was working on projects in Europe. As an incentive, Mr. Green agreed to pay a base salary commensurate with that of beginning evaluators and to provide her with per diem payment at the evaluator rather than the standard operations rate. (But Ms. Andersen would initially have no sales and few bonus income possibilities.) Mr. Green fully intended to help Ms. Andersen move into an evaluator's position at the earliest moment acceptable to the corporation and was confident that this would occur. (See Student Response section for "Decision Point #1," alternatives for Ms. Andersen and Mr. Green.)

"Half a Pie" Remains Half

With these conditions, and assuming that she would be assigned evaluation duties as well as quickly converted to evaluator status, Ms. Andersen accepted Computer Central's offer and was hired as a project manager.

With her extensive technical background, Ms. Andersen was soon in great demand for work on the evaluators teams, under the supervision of various senior evaluators. From February through December of her first year with the company, she worked on projects in Europe. Although she worked on evaluation teams, she was nonetheless designated as a project manager. She was not allowed to make presentations of the technical findings to clients; instead, she was required to write scripts of the senior evaluators' presentations, even in cases for which they lacked the technical expertise to present or explain the information fully. Lacking the official title of evaluator, Ms. Andersen was also not given a team to oversee.

At the end of the year, Ms. Andersen spoke with the head of the European evaluation team, asking for the chance to move into an evaluator's slot. This individual told her that she had to "carry the bags" in order to "earn her wings"—something she felt she had been doing the previous 6 months, and which, to her knowledge, other (male) evaluators had not been required to do. The head of the European team also proposed that she work on an evaluation for a major client who had wanted a technical, rather than a productivity, evaluation, and told her that "This is your shot." At about this time, Ms. Andersen learned from two other female project managers that they, also, had been hired with expectations of moving into evaluator positions.

Ms. Andersen gladly accepted her newest assignment. She soon discovered, however, that a senior and a junior evaluator, neither of whom had any particular technical background, were also assigned to this new technical evaluation. Kirsten worked hard on the project and developed the presentation of the technical aspects the client had requested. She was then excluded from the final two meetings with the client, when the sale was to have taken place. The sale was not made, and Ms. Andersen later was told that she had "blown her chance" to become an evaluator. She reported these developments informally to Mr. Green, who had initially hired her; he continued to believe that an evaluator's position was "just around the corner" for Ms. Andersen. (See Student Response section for "Decision Point #2," alternatives for Ms. Andersen and Mr. Green.)

Pie in the Face

Late in her second year of employment, Computer Central merged with another subsidiary of Techniques Advantage, as part of a general reorganization. At this time, the head of the new European Evaluation unit asked for a list of 10 employees to be converted to evaluators, since technical knowledge was needed for the expanded evaluation team. Because Ms. Andersen was the only employee already working (in other than an evaluator's position) on evaluation teams in Europe, it was widely assumed that she would be selected as one of the 10 new evaluators. Instead, the executive selected 10 men and immediately promoted them to evaluator positions. Of the 2 European selectees, 1 was a programmer and the other a project manager in operations who had repeatedly stated that he had no interest in the high-stress position of evaluator.

Shortly thereafter, Ms. Andersen, at her own request, met with the president of the newly merged firm. She informed him that she had been hired to perform an evaluator's duties and wanted to be appointed to that position. The president acknowledged that there was a "different culture" within Techniques Advantage that needed to be changed and that "he needed strong people like her to help him." He proposed that Ms. Andersen complete an operations installment in the short run and promised that he would confirm with the head of European Evaluation that she would then join the evaluation team as an evaluator. The president informed her later that day that the evaluation team head had said he would be "delighted to have her on his evaluation team, after a little more experience."

Once again, Ms. Andersen agreed. As part of the new arrangement, she was asked to substitute a 3-week home leave rotation for the standard 6-week rotation. To accommodate the company, she agreed to the suggested reduction in home rotation as well.

Ms. Andersen worked effectively on the operations project; in fact, her work set the standard for the other employees with regard to the presentation of analytical material, as well as for structural reorganization and staffing recommendations.

Soon after joining the project, however, she began receiving a series of inaccurate, unusual, and unwarranted memos from Mr. Lawton, head of operations. These memos dealt with minor matters related to her work schedule, such as being an hour late for arrival, even though she and her coworkers did not punch time clocks and routinely worked nights and weekends. In particular, Mr. Lawton criticized her use of her home-leave rotation, even though the 3-week rather than 6-week cycle was undertaken at the request of the company.

Ms. Andersen was sufficiently disturbed by these actions that early in her third year she wrote to Mr. Green and subsequently met with him to discuss her concerns and what action she should pursue next. She was particularly upset about the loss of opportunity and earnings due to being passed over for the evaluators openings and about the recent unwarranted memos. Clearly, some additional action on her part was warranted, but she was uncertain about what course to pursue next. (See Student Response section for "Decision Point #3," alternatives for Ms. Andersen and Mr. Green.)

❖ RELATED READINGS

Bolles, R. (2000). *What color is your parachute? A practical guide for job-hunters and career changers.* Berkeley, CA: Ten Speed Press.

Britton, D. (2000). The epistemology of the gendered organization. *Gender & Society, 11,* 796–818.

Catalyst. (2005). *2005 Catalyst census of women corporate officers and top earners.* New York: Catalyst.

Cobb-Clark, D., & Dunlop, Y. (1999). The role of gender in job promotions. *Monthly Labor Review, 122,* 32–38.

Jacobs, J. A. (1999). The sex segregation of occupations: Prospects for the 21st century. In G. N. Powell (Ed.), *Handbook of gender and work* (pp. 125–141). Thousand Oaks, CA: Sage.

Konrad, A. M., Ritchie, J. E., Lieb, P., & Corrigall, E. (2000). Sex differences and similarities in job attribute preferences: A meta analysis. *Psychological Bulletin, 126,* 593–641.

Marsden, P., & Gorman, E. (2001). Social networks, job changes, and recruitment. In I. Berg and A. L. Kalleberg (Eds.), *Sourcebook of labor markets: Evolving structures and processes* (pp. 467–502). New York: Plenum.

Moore, D. P. (1999). Women entrepreneurs: Approaching a new millennium. In G. N. Powell (Ed.), *Handbook of gender and work* (pp. 371–390). Thousand Oaks, CA: Sage.

Powell, G. N., & Butterfield, D. A. (2002, August). *As the millennium turns: Gender and aspirations to top management.* Paper presented at the meeting of the Academy of Management, Denver, CO.

Powell, G. N., & Parent, J. D. (2002). Gender and managerial stereotypes: Have the times changed? *Journal of Management, 28,* 177–193.

Reskin, B. (2001). Employment discrimination and its remedies. In I. Berg & A. L. Kalleberg (Eds.), *Sourcebook of labor markets: Evolving structures and process* (pp. 567–599). New York: Plenum.

Reskin, B., & Padavic, I. (2002). *Women and men at work.* Thousand Oaks, CA: Pine Forge Press.

Twomey, D. (1990). *Equal employment opportunity law.* Chicago: South-Western.

U.S. Equal Employment Opportunity Commission. (2002). *A new look through the glass ceiling: Where are the women?* Washington, DC: U.S. General Accounting Office.

Wind, A. (1995). *Demand letter for client.* Washington, DC: Wind & Associates.

❖ STUDENT RESPONSE

Decision Point #1: The Job Offer

1. Assume the role of Mr. Green, who has been told that "women don't throw themselves into their work enough" to be evaluators. Why doesn't Mr. Green confront his superior, CEO Charles, with the issue of sexual stereotyping of the evaluator's position? If you chose to confront the issue at this point, how might you do so?

2. Assume the role of the job applicant, Ms. Andersen. Should Ms. Andersen accept this lower-level position, even though executives

of Computer Central seem to agree she is qualified for the evaluator's job for which she has applied? What advantages would you consider at this point?

Decision Point #2: Initial Experience in the Firm

1. Assume the role of Ms. Andersen. After encountering sexual stereotypes in the type of work and presentations you are allowed to engage in, and in the light of similar treatment of several other women, what major action alternatives can you identify? Which of these do you prefer, and why?

2. Assume the role of Mr. Green. Ms. Andersen has spoken to you about her frustrations with sexual stereotyping in her assignments and about similar experiences of several other women. How might you affect the climate of the organization on these matters? Describe some specific alternatives you would consider.

Decision Point #3: After Evaluators' Positions Are Awarded to Men

1. Assume the role of Ms. Andersen. Should you continue your responsibilities, hoping for an evaluator's position later, resign, pursue legal action, or some combination of these options? Justify the action you recommend, using information from the case.

2. What evidence of sex discrimination is there in this case? (Consult the Appendix for the case.)

3. Assume the role of Mr. Green. Identify your alternatives, should Ms. Andersen pursue legal remedies. Which of these do you prefer, and why?

APPENDIX: TITLE VII OF THE CIVIL RIGHTS ACT OF 1964

The following sections are taken directly from Title VII of the Civil Rights Act of 1964 (Public Law 88–352) as it appears in volume 42 of the United States Code, beginning at section 2000e. Title VII prohibits employment discrimination based on race, color, religion, sex and national origin.

Under this law, companies employing fifteen or more people are prevented from discriminating in the areas of

- Hiring and firing
- Compensation and promotion
- Transfer or layoff
- Job advertisement and recruitment
- Testing
- Training and apprenticeship programs
- Use of company facilities
- Fringe benefits, retirement plans, and disability leave

The Civil Rights Act of 1991 (Public Law 102–166) amends several sections of Title VII related to the proving of the "disparate impact" of employer's actions on different groups of employees, and the awarding of damages in such cases. The Equal Pay Act is another amendment to Title VII; it requires that an employer pay all employees equally for equal work, regardless of gender. The law covers situations where men and women perform jobs that require equal skill, effort, and responsibility. The exception to this law is a pay system that is based on a factor other than gender, such as seniority, or the quantity or quality of items produced or processed.

An employer is expected to post notices describing the federal laws prohibiting job discrimination based on race, color, sex, national origin, religion, age, and disability and describing the provisions of the Equal Pay Act. The Equal Employment Opportunity Commission was created in the 1964 Civil Rights Act to investigate and, if necessary, prosecute in court violations of the employment provisions of the law. The EEOC publishes clear guidelines on how to file complaints of employment discrimination.

Unlawful Employment Practices
(Title VII, 1964 Civil Rights Act)

SEC. 2000e-2. (Section 703)

(a) It shall be an unlawful employment practice for an employer—

1. to fail or refuse to hire or to discharge any individual, or otherwise to discriminate against any individual with respect to

his compensation, terms, conditions, or privileges of employment, because of such individual's race, color, religion, sex, or national origin; or

2. to limit, segregate, or classify his employees or applicants for employment in any way which would deprive or tend to deprive any individual of employment opportunities or otherwise adversely affect his status as an employee, because of such individual's race, color, religion, sex, or national origin.

(b) It shall be an unlawful employment practice for an employment agency to fail or refuse to refer for employment, or otherwise to discriminate against, any individual because of his race, color, religion, sex, or national origin, or to classify or refer for employment any individual on the basis of his race, color, religion, sex, or national origin.

(c) It shall be an unlawful employment practice for any employer, labor organization, or joint labor-management committee controlling apprenticeship or other training or retraining, including on-the-job training programs, to discriminate against any individual because of his race, color, religion, sex, or national origin in admission to, or employment in, any program established to provide apprenticeship or other training.

2

One Step Forward, Two Steps Back?

CASE OVERVIEW

The primary subject matter of this case concerns career development and career choices of female professionals in contemporary China, with details from the period since the Cultural Revolution (1970s). The case centers on the experience of a woman educated for diplomatic service and teaching, who at the end of the case is offered a choice of moving to a joint-venture business. Major content relates to gender roles interacting with career choices. Secondary topics include changes in the structure of the Chinese economy and government policies related to marriage and family. Comparisons can be drawn between gender expectations and work-family issues in China and those in other cultures with which students are familiar.

❖ BODY OF CASE

Jin Xiaoqin reached for a sip of her herbal tea and tried to calm herself. Her life had built in a steady crescendo to a point of decision and, like many Chinese women, the reality of having the power to make serious life choices was both new and anxiety-producing. So far, she reflected, her story had been a largely fortunate one.

Born to rural parents in the early years of the People's Republic, her initial expectations had been modest. She dutifully attended school, even into the second and third levels not usually completed by girls, especially in rural, mountainous areas such as hers. Now, of course, things were different in China, and more girls were enrolled in school. In preprimary education, 88 girls were enrolled for every 100 boys in 1995; the ratio was 90 to 100 in early primary grades but dropped to 66 girls for every 100 boys in second level; data are unavailable for the third level, precollege training (United Nations, 1999). But in the 1960s the idea of girls pursuing education had still been unusual; Jin had encountered resistance and even censure in her small farm community, but because her parents had supported her aspirations, she had continued. She knew their encouragement was in part due to the lack of a son, which would have made them far happier, and she did her best to compensate by achieving to the best of her abilities.

Completion of the third level, of course, usually meant admission to college, though the field of study and the institution of enrollment were traditionally selected by formal testing and procedures rather than by the choice of individual students and their families. In the 1970s, however, the Cultural Revolution had gripped China. The college admissions tests had been suspended between 1970 and 1976, leaving only two avenues into college: waiting until the exams would be given again (which did occur in 1978) or being selected for college as a "peasant scholar." Jin Xiaoqin fortunately fell into the latter category.

Jin was at that time part of a farm cooperative, near the village of Caijiacun, about 200 miles from the capital of Jiangxi Province, her home community. (Later, in the 1990s, the youth of this community left it in massive numbers to pursue better opportunities in the eastern cities of China.) In the early 1970s, however, all remained at home, struggling to eke out a living in the impoverished farm village. Further, many urban youth were sent to rural areas such as Jiangxi Province, with the goal of increasing their understanding of the rural peasant's life. Jin's village friend, Cai Songquan, longed to move away from the area but was not allowed to leave because he was an only son and the sole provider for aging parents. Some of her friends from the city did not really survive their rural experience with their educational motivation intact; rather, they faded into relative obscurity, sometimes marrying and remaining in their transplanted or originally rural lives, or returning to the cities with less lofty aspirations, identifying more completely with the working masses of their country.

Jin counted herself lucky to return to her previous status as a student by being admitted to the foreign studies college in Beijing. There the key faculty and administrators determined that her major area should be English with a second concentration in international relations. (The "worker-peasant scholars" of this period were given no choice in their areas of study.) Secretly, Jin hoped for a career in China's diplomatic corps, but she realized that such ambitions must be subdued and contained within the goals and positions established for her by the state. She entered into her college experience enthusiastically and gratefully, competing fiercely for grades and accomplishments that would enhance her future.

While in college Jin met and fell in love with Gong Liu, another student of international affairs with aspirations to government service. Gong was an outgoing and ambitious young man, though his academic achievements were not as compelling as Jin's. After graduation the two married and were both assigned to the Chinese Foreign Service. Jin was encouraged to accept a teaching position at the Foreign Affairs College, where excellent teachers, also members of the foreign service, taught future foreign service recruits. Educated workers had somewhat more choices in China by this time. Before economic reform in 1978, labor mobility, employment, and wage levels in China were fully controlled by the government, and no one had a choice over the type of work to undertake. After 1978, however, the educated groups could choose the privately controlled enterprises and even, as in Jin's case, have some choices if they were still in a government cadre of workers (Meng, 1998, p. 69). Jin was happy about her teaching opportunity because the teachers received far better housing assignments than did the rank-and-file diplomats while in Beijing. Jin had a small, heavily subsidized, basic apartment with private bath, while single diplomats were assigned to shared quarters.

Gong, who entered the diplomatic corps at the same time, was aware that his housing was superior to that of his colleagues only because he was married to Jin. While enjoying the better accommodations and lifestyle, he felt diminished to have received this benefit through his wife. Even after the Revolution in the 1940s, many Chinese retained their traditional views of gender roles, and Gong shared many of these opinions. Traditionally, Chinese men expected to be the major providers and to have their spouses and families dependent and grateful to them; women had no authority or say in the management of important family matters, nor should they participate as individuals in social, political, and economic activities. Although greater access to education and employment outside the home had resulted in significant improvements in the status of Chinese women, particularly in the eastern urban centers, the traditional values and norms that had relegated women to an inferior position within the family and in society continued to prevail among many social groups in China (United Nations, 1998, p. 13). Clearly Jin's role as faculty at a respected institution was somewhat threatening to Gong, and some tension in the marriage resulted from her privileges.

Early in her faculty appointment, Jin also began study to obtain her master's degree, really a necessity in order to fully secure her teaching position. Her status among faculty had originally been somewhat reduced by her never having taken the college entrance exam. Receiving her master's fully established her academic credibility among the faculty. Gong also enrolled in graduate studies. Jin completed her master's degree first, another development that was not particularly pleasing to her husband.

Gong also began to receive assignments abroad. At first they were short, usually only a few months at a time. Soon, however, he was assigned to a 2-year posting in an embassy abroad. There was little question of Jin accompanying him, since families of diplomats below the rank of counselor generally were expected to remain in China. Single men were welcome in postings abroad, but unmarried women were not; it was believed that single women could too easily be compromised in an international setting. They could not have a normal social life, because rumors about them might jeopardize their reputations and thus harm the foreign policy undertakings of their embassy. They could also, it was felt, be subjected to blackmail. In addition, it was common knowledge that women were less hardy and less able to adjust to foreign cultures and the demands of living overseas. Thus, single and married men were greatly preferred for foreign postings. Service abroad was clearly "man's work," and Gong and Jin accepted that they would live apart much of the time. This was only to be expected. These attitudes also affected Jin's decision to stay in teaching rather than pursuing her original dream of a foreign service career.

Jin meanwhile was doing well at her college. Women were a minority among the faculty in the early 1980s, since few women completed the necessary education. Among members of the diplomatic corps, however, teaching positions were highly desired by women who did qualify because they appreciated the housing benefits and the greater flexibility of hours and assignments than mainstream diplomats had.

Jin and Gong conceived a child, and their son, Yuan, was born in 1986. Because of the one-child policy, the couple had strictly practiced birth control until deciding to conceive their child. (They were totally in tune with their generation on this matter; 72% of Chinese females of childbearing age practiced modern birth control in 1983, and 83% by 1990) (United Nations, 1998, p. 23.) The one-child policy was strictly adhered to by anyone in government service, so the couple was grateful that their child was a son. Legislation stipulated that urban couples should generally have only one child and violators faced fines. As of the turn of the century, China reported that the one-child policy had been responsible for preventing 300 million births in the previous 20 years and is still essential to avoiding a population explosion and starvation (BBC News, 2002). The birthrate has clearly declined since the policy began. As loyal government employees, there was no question whether Jin and Gong would have only this child.

Jin was able to spend time with the infant initially, but shortly she returned to her teaching. All four of Yuan's grandparents were happy to care for the child when his parents had work responsibilities. Often in China the lack of child-care programs made working difficult for mothers, but this was more the case among the less educated groups. Jin was able to see Yuan after her teaching hours ended and enjoyed somewhat more time with him than did some of her friends in office-bound positions. Gong loved the boy but regarded planning and arranging for his care as his wife's responsibility. When Yuan reached school age he was admitted to a public kindergarten, and he even had a nursery school available the year before kindergarten.

Jin left China when Yuan was 1 year old, to study for a year at Harvard University, in the Fletcher School of Law and Diplomacy, one of the highest-ranked international relations programs in the United States. Graduate study in the United States was highly valued, for both the education itself and the greater understanding of Westerners it provided. In the Chinese diplomatic corps, such opportunities were very competitive and highly prized. While Jin was away, Yuan resided with his mother's parents, a common arrangement for Chinese parents who are assigned overseas.

In the United States Jin lectured some and also collaborated with political scientists at the university. She grew in confidence and in her competence in the English language. After her return, her English was rated at the highest level, a skill that usually would place her in important overseas work at Chinese embassies in Western countries. But Jin remained in her teaching post in order to keep the security and benefits it provided and avoid the stress and problems encountered by female Chinese diplomats seeking overseas postings. Jin also knew that if she sought overseas assignments, she and Gong would very likely be posted to different countries and not encouraged to take Yuan with either of them. While his grandparents would care for him whenever necessary, Jin did not want to be separated from her son so regularly.

After another decade of teaching, however, Jin again had occasion to study in the United States, this time at the University of Virginia. She pursued graduate work in English and also taught in collaboration with faculty there. Again her skills and confidence increased, and she returned happy that she had taken the opportunity.

Jin found China much changed in the mid-1990s. Women accounted for 45% of the total workforce and 40% of the total industrial labor force; about 22% of the members of the Chinese parliament were female, a higher percentage than in most countries of the region (United Nations, 1999, pp. 151, 174). About 32% of all government employees were female by 1994 (United Nations, 1998, p. 58). However, in the ministerial ranks of government, including the high-level foreign policy positions of most interest to Jin and Gong, fewer than 10% were female. Most of the women in the ministerial ranks (about 62%) were entrusted with social affairs, such as social services and welfare, health, education, and women's affairs; they were rare in the economic development field or in foreign policy and defense-related positions (United Nations, 1998, p. 67).

An increase in privatization had opened many opportunities for the educated class, as joint ventures between Chinese and Western companies entered the economic scene, and political and economic reforms allowed Chinese to make more professional choices on their own, to buy their own apartments, and for some fortunate ones to make substantial incomes they had only dreamed of previously. Women in urban areas were still better educated than in rural areas; in Beijing, 73% of working women now had a high school degree and 17% had a university education (Shaffer, Joplin, Bell, Lau, & Oguz, 2000b). Despite progress in the Chinese mainland organizations, however, women were employed in 50% fewer professional jobs and about 11% of the managerial jobs in which men were employed (Honh, 1995). By the mid-1990s there was an abundant workforce, and 73% of women 15 years old and older were economically active. Jin realized that in the rural areas most of these benefits were not yet realized and that education was the reason for the new opportunities she saw. Even in the countryside, primary school dropout rates for girls had decreased to between 3 and 5%, an improvement, though the size of the population meant a large number of women remained uneducated (Dowd, 1995; United Nations, 1998, p. 39).

Gong was more often spending his time abroad, and the couple grew apart. Shortly after Jin's return they formally separated, though neither seemed immediately motivated toward a divorce. Formal separation from her husband actually made little impact on Jin's life, since the couple had been often apart and both Jin and son Yuan were accustomed to this. Jin did realize, though, that China's new laws gave her certain formal rights, such as those found in the new marriage law of 2001. The new law outlawed married people living with an opposite gender person not their spouse. Further, a man found guilty of divorcing his wife to live with his mistress can be sued by his former wife for financial compensation. This prompted many lawsuits. The Chinese Supreme Court ruled in 2002 that simply having affairs or keeping a concubine was *not* covered by the new law, which narrowed the law's application (Changes, 2002). It remained to be seen if any of this might become relevant, should Jin and Gong decide to divorce.

Yuan, now a bright and self-sufficient teenager and level-three student, required less and less of Jin's time and energy. Her parents, however, were becoming elderly and increasingly dependent on her, their only child, both financially and emotionally. No public support really existed that would ensure their care as they continued to age. Jin also felt increasing pressure to further develop her personal life and opportunities on her own, particularly after her separation from Gong. She became involved in a variety of community groups and sought responsibility on the neighborhood council of her urban community. She was also part of a wider movement toward political participation among Chinese women at this time. In 2002 the newspaper *People's Daily,* a voice of the government, clearly called for more such efforts to push women's rights, stating: "More women should participate in the deliberation and administration of State affairs. More female cadres should be trained, selected and play a role at various levels. In this way women can better enjoy their political rights" (What They Are Saying, 2002, p. 4).

Challenging work in this capacity brought home the realization that she was stagnating a bit at the university. Her job was secure, yes, but also lacking in challenge. She had been easily promoted to associate professor and anticipated no difficulty in achieving the highest rank of full professor. Since she had not served for more than a few weeks at embassies abroad, however, she could not aspire to policymaking or top administrative roles at her college, all of which required actual foreign service experience abroad. Many of her college contemporaries were advancing and exploring new opportunities, some in the foreign service and others in the private joint ventures that were thriving in the new economic structure. But women were still disadvantaged in the Chinese Foreign Service. As of 2002 about 4,000 staff members were included in the Foreign Ministry, among which about 1,200 were female cadres, with 800 based in the ministry and only 400 on foreign posts. Of those assigned abroad, 45 held the rank of counselor or above; 6 of these were ambassadors, 5 counsels-general.

As she sat on her rooftop this sunny May morning, Jin considered the meeting she had had last week with a cousin who was part of the executive team of a new joint venture in electronics with an American firm. The enterprise was expanding very rapidly, with more need for middle managers and technical staff competent in English. Xin Meng had called Jin and asked to meet to discuss hiring her as a vice president for staff development. The salary would be triple her current one, and there would be frequent trips to the United States, which Jin always enjoyed. Still, she would need to give up her years of accrued seniority, her comfortable and subsidized housing, and most important, her job security. Jin knew of many, such as her engineering friend Liu, who had ventured forth into the newly emerging private sector only to be unemployed and scrambling for an income a few years later—when economic developments or the inexperienced management of the new enterprises brought severe downturns or even collapse of the ventures. The Western partners, of course, also suffered in these events but could absorb the losses far more easily than the new entrepreneurs within China itself. The political and legal systems, also, were just beginning to address many issues of a partially free market, and individual workers and companies were often at risk for lack of a stable legal framework.

Thus, even in the new China, Jin realized there were hurdles that professional women would encounter (Shaffer, Joplin, Bell, Lau, & Oguz, 2000a). The Chinese mainland has a long history of equal-rights legislation; the first constitution (1954) provided women with equal rights with men in economic, cultural, social, and family arenas. Insofar as this is more a statement of intent than a guarantee of rights (Pearson 1995), several amendments, including the Law on Safeguarding the Rights and Interests of Women (1992), have been designed to further guarantee women's rights and promote equality with men. However, Jin knew that these amendments have been criticized for lack of penalties and general imprecision. Indeed, despite legal protections, differential treatment of women and sexual harassment in the

People's Republic of China still seemed widespread (Honh, 1995). Further, conditions are worse for women in the countryside, where 75% of Chinese women still resided in 2000 (Rural Women, 2002).

The recent economic reforms have stressed efficiency, and women have been discriminated against in hiring, layoffs, and wage and pension systems (Summerfield, 1994; Zheng, 1995). Sexual harassment has increased, especially among rural women moving to urban areas, where they suffer exploitation and harassment (Jacka, 1997; Zhong, 1994). Movement from a planned, controlled economy to a market economy has also resulted in loss of administrative controls and protections, which have been replaced by personal wishes and rule of managers, the majority (89%) of whom are male (Honh, 1995). A study by the All-China Women's Federation Research Institute had shown that "Women's mobility in their life-long career tends to be horizontal while men's mobility is upward" (Zheng, 1995, p. 73). In layoffs, the proportion of laid-off female workers has been higher (59%) than that of male workers (Zhang & Zhao, cited in Cooke, 2001). This research also found that women were discriminated against in retirement and often compelled to retire at an earlier age than men. Thus, Jin feared she might have more long-term security risk in a private-sector position. She could see that the new saying about women's overall progress in China, "one step forward, two steps back," might apply to her.

All her life others had made most of the choices: her work in the countryside, her matriculation at a particular college, the choice of her fields of study, even her assignments to study in the United States had primarily been dictates of her government. She recalled how, in college, she had dreamed of a diplomatic career that had never materialized for her; she knew that, had she been male, she would have pursued assignments with the Foreign Service abroad. Now, in the middle of her life, the new economic and political conditions in China presented her with a serious professional alternative and a somewhat frightening choice. What should she do?

❖ RELATED READINGS

BBC News. (2002, January 9). *Concern at Chinese family planning law.* London: Author.

Changes in China's marriage law in 2001. (2002, January 5). *China News Digest.*

Cooke, F. L. (2001). Equal opportunity? The role of legislation and public policies in women's employment in China. *Women in Management Review, 16*(7), 334–348.

Dowd, S. (1995). Women and the word: The silencing of the feminine. In J. Peters & A. Wolper (Eds.), *Women's rights/human rights* (pp. 317–323). New York: Routledge.

Honh, Z. (1995). The testimony of women writers: The situation of women in China today. In J. Peters & A. Wolper (Eds.), *Women's rights/human rights* (pp. 96–100). New York: Routledge.

Jacka, T. (1997). *Women's work in rural China: Change and continuity in an era of reform.* Cambridge, UK: Cambridge University Press.

Louie, K. (2002). *Theorizing Chinese masculinity: Society and gender in China.* Cambridge, UK: Cambridge University Press.

Meng, X. (1998). Male-female wage determination and gender discrimination in China's rural industrial sector. *Labour Economics, 5*, 67–89.

Pearson, V. (1995). Goods on which one loses: Women and mental health in China. *Social Science Medicine, 41*, 1159–1173.

Rural women sample state affairs. (2002, May 14). *China Daily,* p. 10.

Shaffer, M. A., Joplin, J. R. W., Bell, M. P., Lau, T., & Oguz, C. (2000a). Disruptions to women's social identity: A comparative study of workplace stress experienced by women in three geographic regions. *Journal of Occupational Health Psychology, 5*(4), 441–456.

Shaffer, M. A., Joplin, J. R. W., Bell, M. P., Lau, T., & Oguz, C. (2000b). Gender discrimination and job-related outcomes: A cross-cultural comparison of working women in the United States and China. *Journal of Vocational Behavior, 57*, 395–427.

Summerfield, G. (1994). Economic reform and the employment of Chinese women. *Journal of Economic Issues, 28*(3), 715–732.

United Nations. Economic and Social Commission. (1998). *Women and men in the ESCAP region.* New York: Author.

United Nations. Economic and Social Commission. (1999). *Statistics on women in Asia and the Pacific, 1999.* New York: Author.

What they are saying: Protecting women's rights. (2002, May 11). *China Daily,* p. 4.

Xin, F. (1995). The Chinese cultural system: Implications for cross-cultural management. *SAM Advanced Management Journal, 60*, 14–20.

Zhang, H. X. (1999). Female migration and urban labour markets in Tianjin. *Development and Change, 30*(1), 21–41.

Zhang, M., & Zhao, L. L. (1999). The situations of labour protection for female workers in Guangdong Province. *China National Conditions and Strength, 12*, 37.

Zheng, X.-Y. (1995). *Zhong-guo nu xing ren kou wen it yu fa zhan* [The problem of Chinese women population and its development]. Beijing: Beijing University Press.

Zhong, J. (1994). *Zhong-guo xing sao rao xian xiang ji dui ce* [Sexual harassment of women in China and its coping strategies]. Sichuan: Sichuan People.

❖ STUDENT RESPONSE

1. What were the most important gender expectations shaping Jin's early life in China? What can you see changing in China during the years of Jin's career as described in the case?

2. What key family policies affected Jin's career path? What changes would have increased her choices earlier in her career? Why do you suppose China did not institute these changes?

3. How is her marriage important to the developments in Jin's life and career? How is this similar to or different from similar issues in the United States or other Western societies?

4. Do some research on the U.S. Foreign Service. How would the career of a female U.S. diplomat be similar to and different from what Jin experienced from the 1980s to the present time?

5. What are the key factors in Jin's upcoming decision? From what you know about her and about contemporary China, what do you think she would choose, and why?

APPENDIX: EXCERPTS FROM THE POPULATION AND FAMILY PLANNING LAW OF THE PEOPLE'S REPUBLIC OF CHINA

Chapter III. Regulation of Reproduction

Article 17. Citizens have the right to reproduction as well as the obligation to practice family planning according to law. Both husband and wife bear equal responsibility for family planning.

Article 18. The State maintains its current policy for reproduction, encouraging late marriage and childbearing and advocating one child per couple. Where the requirements specified by laws and regulations are met, plans for a second child, if requested, may be made. Specific measures in this regard shall be formulated by the people's congress. . . .

Family planning shall also be introduced to the ethnic peoples.

Article 19. Family planning shall be practiced chiefly by means of contraception.

The State shall create conditions to ensure that individual citizens knowingly choose safe, effective, and appropriate contraceptive methods.

Article 20. Couples of reproductive age shall conscientiously adopt contraceptive methods and accept technical services and guidance for family planning.

Incidence of unwanted pregnancies shall be prevented and reduced.

Article 21. Couples of reproductive age who practice family planning shall receive, free of charge, the basic items of technical services specified by the State.

The funds needed for rendering the services specified in the preceding paragraph shall, in accordance with relevant State regulations, be listed in the budget or be guaranteed by social insurance plans.

Article 22. Discrimination against and maltreatment of women who give birth to baby girls or who suffer from infertility are prohibited.

Discrimination against, maltreatment of, and abandonment of baby girls are prohibited.

SOURCE: Population and Family Planning Law of the People's Republic of China. Legislative Affairs Commission of the Standing Committee of the National People's Congress of the People's Republic of China, China Population Publishing House, 2002.

3

Did Attorney Evans Bump Her Head on the "Glass Ceiling"?

CASE OVERVIEW

This case describes the problems that a seemingly well qualified female attorney in a prestigious law firm experienced in obtaining a partnership. The process the firm uses to decide on admitting a firm member to partnership is documented. Issues related to gender discrimination in professional advancement, particularly the glass ceiling phenomenon and the informal organizational culture, are the focus of the case. Policies of the firm, sample evaluations of the attorney, and some policy recommendations to firms from the American Bar Association are all included as supporting material in the appendices, as are the instructions for filing sex discrimination claims with the Equal Employment Opportunity Commission (EEOC).

❖ BODY OF CASE

Meghan Evans sat stunned in her friend Margot's apartment. Just that afternoon she learned that the Associates Committee in her law firm planned to recommend against considering her for partnership. This was only the latest negative experience for her at work; her entire seven-year history with the firm had been somewhat troubled.

Background

Meghan Evans managed, despite the added responsibilities of raising two children on her own, to complete law school with an out-standing record. Widely recruited by prestigious firms, and highly ambitious, she settled upon Wilson, Barnes, Sauer and Kahn, a firm of more than 200 attorneys. Her goal was to be a successful trial attorney, and she served in the litigation department of Wilson, Barnes. After seven years, Ms. Evans's superiors in the Litigation Department, with whom she had seven most closely, wanted her to be named a partner in the firm.

In recent years the firm, like many nationally, had toughened its standards for achieving partner status. Firms cannot afford partners who are unable to pay their own way, and many expect their partners to work very hard indeed. Women continue to have a harder time than men in achieving partnership, and many more women than men resign from large firms out of discouragement before reaching the number of years required (American Bar Association [ABA], 2001). While Meghan's firm overall had few women partners, there were several in the litigation department, though none in the area of corporate litigation. All the female litigation partners had opted for the firm's part-time partnerships. One of the two female equity partners (of a total of 55 equity partners), the highest rank in the firm, had children but complained she never saw them. The requirements of the firm to be "on call," and the difficulty of combining the hours requirement for partnership with the demands of a family were considerable.

Just last year the firm had raised its hours requirement—the number of billable hours to achieve bonuses as an associate and a standard for those seeking eventual partnership—to 2000 hours, the highest requirement among the major firms in her city. "We have to be 'lean and mean' in the current business environment," argued a partner with whom Meghan worked frequently. "You might as well get used to these hours, if this is the career you want."

Meghan loved her work in corporate litigation, but she also wanted and needed some predictability of hours and flexibility to meet the needs of her family and to have a personal life. Nationally, her age cohort of young associates shared her concerns; many of them would gladly have taken substantial pay reductions in order to work fewer hours and not be on call every evening and weekend (ABA, 2001).

The firm had policies that seemed to allow both men and women to advance. A number of women had achieved partner status, though none in corporate law; the work culture required that attorneys dealing with business clients be on call, and the work frequently involved long hours and extended travel to other metropolitan areas. The firm's policies allowed for part-time partners; Meghan knew several women who had received these positions. Technically they worked fewer hours (30–35 hours per week, normally), but in practice they were often called in and sent on business trips just like full-time attorneys. Their arrangements called for a percentage of work over a year—60% of a full partner's hours, for example—but in practice they were required to finish any cases they had begun, to come in frequently on off days, even if doing so resulted in more hours worked than their contract required. "Do you think it is worth it?" Meghan had asked one of the female part-timers. "Yes, it is to me," the friend responded. "Even though I work far more than my agreement stipulates, I always know I will have no trouble in meeting my stated hours requirement." Meghan found this picture of "just as much work but less compensation" really unfair.

Pregnancy and family leave, as well as four weeks of paid vacation, were also policies on the books at Wilson, Barnes. In fact, though, Meghan's friend Anne reported that she experienced great difficulties after her pregnancy leave. "The partner who took on my clients refused to funnel all of the work back to me, after my return," Anne complained. "After the baby was born, I never regained the same referral status, in terms of getting prime assignments that I had before my pregnancy leave. So technically I was back at the firm, but in actuality I was receiving very different treatment." Anne subsequently left the firm for another position, following the example of many female associates, who have a much higher attrition rate from major firms than do men (National Association for Legal Practice, 2003). All six of the other female associates in Meghan's division during her time there had resigned for various reasons. Obviously this high resignation rate was one contributor to the small number of women partners in the firm.

Meghan also remembered the times she had felt excluded from some of the informal occasions that can lead to higher visibility and assignments in the firm, through social networking. One summer all the associates in the corporate division of the firm had gone on a weekend retreat to a resort area; the stated purpose of the event was team building by spending informal time together. Told the event would end Saturday, Meghan and another female associate made plans to return to the city. During a meal conversation, they discovered that all the men had been invited to stay for an additional day of golf. On several other occasions, Meghan felt unable to attend evening social events because of family commitments.

While having to pass up attending such events may appear merely annoying, the events can in fact create personal networks in the firm that advantaged some associates, perhaps at the expense of others. On one of her major cases involving out-of-town court work, Meghan had not been invited to accompany the team, even though her work had figured prominently in the case's development. The supervisor told her, "Well, you know, I just knew this other guy's availability and I wasn't sure of yours." Getting credit for acquiring clients for the firm was another issue in which she felt men often were favored; women working with clients were sometimes seen as providing for the "care and feeding of clients," a phrase that somewhat downgraded their client relations. "If a guy is going for a game of golf, he is free to just say that; somehow if I say I have a family commitment, some perceive it as a lack of commitment to the firm," Meghan complained.

As her friend James points out, though, men who value family time may suffer even more informal discrimination in firms. "Only about 4% of all lawyers in a national study had ever worked part-time, and there is some evidence that men doing so rarely make partner," James asserted (Noonan & Corcoran, 2004). "When I took 12 weeks of parental leave when Jared was born, there were a lot of raised eyebrows among the partners, and no adjustment was made to my billable hours requirement that year, even though the leave was firm policy and fully compensated." "Yes," Meghan responded. "We are both caught in the same gendered trap . . . with me sometimes being punished by the assumption that my family makes me 'cheat' the firm, and you for taking fatherhood as seriously as your career."

The Firm's Evaluation

The evaluation process to become a full partner at Wilson, Barnes, as in many large firms, was complex. It relied on personal networking and having the respect of existing partners—often heavily influenced by the visibility and importance of the cases to which the associate had been assigned—as well as an assessment of a portfolio of hundreds of written evaluations of her work. In these portfolio evaluations, those working with the attorney in question scored her in 20 categories and also gave her an overall performance rating or score. Associates within two years of being considered for partnership were reviewed annually; less senior associates were evaluated semiannually. Aside from rumors, associates were never told how the results of their evaluations were arrived at, how the various factors might be weighted, or who served on the associates committee that recommended partners to the Executive Committee. Partners argued that this secrecy was necessary to prevent inappropriate lobbying for partnership status.

In the year an associate became eligible for partnership consideration, she was asked to name the five partners for whom she had done the most work in each of the previous 3 years. These partners received a detailed questionnaire, and the results were compiled by another partner, who presented them to the Associates Committee. The process attempted to recognize that successful attorneys need to be evaluated in a wide variety of areas, using a composite picture of their talents rather than a single attribute or skill, since no associate can achieve the highest level in each of the established criteria. (The reality is that some associates do certain things better than others, and the process forces each to be evaluated as an individual.)

Ten criteria of legal performance were listed on the forms: legal analysis, legal writing and drafting, research skills, formal speech, informal speech, judgment, creativity, negotiating and advocacy, promptness, and efficiency. Ten personal characteristics were also evaluated: reliability, taking and managing responsibility, flexibility, growth potential, attitude, client relationship, client servicing and development, ability under pressure, ability to work independently, and dedication.

Partners provided grades as well as written comments on these criteria. The evaluation forms described the grades as follows:

1. *Distinguished:* Outstanding, exceptional; consistently demonstrates extraordinary adeptness and quality; star.

2. *Good:* Displays particular merit on a consistent basis; effective work product and performance; able; talented.

3. *Acceptable:* Satisfactory; adequate; displays neither particular merit nor any serious defects or omissions; dependable.

4. *Marginal:* Inconsistent work product and performance; *sometimes* below the level of what you expect from associates.

5. *Unacceptable:* Fails to meet minimum standard of quality expected of an associate at this level; *frequently* below the acceptable level.

Evaluating partners were also asked to describe any particular strengths or weaknesses of an associate. In addition, partners were told to indicate their views on the admission of each senior associate to the partnership, among these five choices: "with enthusiasm," "with favor," "with mixed emotions," "with negative feelings," and "no opinion." Finally, partners were asked to respond yes or no to the following general question: "I would feel comfortable turning over to this associate to handle on his/her own a significant matter for one of my clients." In addition to recommendations of partners and the evaluation of portfolios, the review process included some quantitative measures of performance, such as hours billed, business generated, new business attracted to the firm, and so on.

Partners other than those for whom the attorney had worked the most were also allowed to submit evaluations if they wished. This happens informally, at a series of breakfast discussions. The review of the associate's record, including the evaluations submitted by all partners who cared to do so, was initially conducted by a 10-partner Associates Committee; with their favorable partnership recommendation, the matter was reviewed by a five-member Executive Committee, which makes recommendations to the entire group of partners, numbering 94 at the time of Ms. Evans's consideration. While the Executive Committee *usually* ratifies the choices of the Associates Committee, they are not required to do so. In any case, only those associates nominated by the Executive Committee would be presented to the entire partnership for a vote. The final vote of all the partners, while it is made to appear very democratic, is actually quite well controlled by the two committees making the recommendations; they lobby partners to support their choices, and all partners know who is being recommended.

Meghan had anticipated that her partnership seemed almost a foregone conclusion at Wilson, Barnes. Her superiors in the litigation department wanted her as a partner. They admired and respected her work, and they liked her as a person. In addition, in respect to the portfolio evaluation system, Meghan's reviews from the partners for whom she had done substantial work were consistently positive for the entire 7 years of her service. While such matters are obviously subjective and difficult to measure, she believed that a majority of the partners in the firm clearly seemed to respond favorably to her, both personally and professionally.

Despite this seemingly rosy picture, the 10-partner Associates Committee had just recommended, by a vote of 9 to 1, against Meghan Evans's acceptance as full partner. They did, however, recommend to the Executive Committee that she be offered a special partnership (terms undefined) in the domestic relations department of the firm, a unit from which two partners were leaving the firm, and where they believed her skills would be most useful. The Associates Committee suggested that she might be able to make full partnership relatively soon in this department because of the positive evaluations she received on work with clients and in the courtroom.

The field of domestic relations has often been one of the most available specialties for women attorneys; Meghan believed she was being told that she must practice in the "women's part" of the firm. Further, given the nature of modern marriages, this work presents complex legal issues. The analytical skills required are daunting, especially with regard to the taxation issues involved. Thus, Ms. Evans, with 6 years of experience in business litigation, believed that she lacked the requisite background for the domestic relations work.

It was this news that Meghan had just received that afternoon.

Meghan's Legal Argument

"I just cannot decide what to do next," Meghan said to her friend Margot, an employment attorney. Margot and Meghan agreed that her denial of partnership constituted discrimination on the basis of sex. Meghan recalled many indications of such possible discrimination. "In my initial job interview with the firm," she remembered," a partner told me it would not be easy for me at Wilson because I 'was a woman, had not attended an Ivy League law school, and had not been on law review.'" Meghan also felt, at times, that she was given less desirable assignments, with less visibility, than her male counterparts received. "I think this probably has affected my evaluations from partners who have not had direct contact with me," she said.

Meghan also could provide specific crude and unprofessional statements made by one of the firm's male attorneys to female attorneys that demonstrated a work environment hostile to women. One corporate partner was widely known for attending strip clubs while on business travel and making frequent remarks about that to women attorneys also making the trips; several women had complained, but the behavior continued. He had circulated pictures of himself at the Playboy mansion to colleagues at work. On one occasion Meghan had been yelled at and had documents thrown at her by a male colleague with a bullying style. She confronted this behavior, and the colleague replied that it was common at the firm and she should get used to it. (Later, however, this colleague had been reprimanded and voluntarily left the firm.)

"I think you can prove discrimination here," said her friend Margot. "You would need to prove that the reason given for your denial—lack of sufficient legal analysis ability, was really a cover or pretext for gender discrimination. You'd also need to point out the instances in which your male colleagues were treated differently from how you were in the evaluation process. Since the evaluation is essentially a subjective one, we should be able to show how influenced it might be by gender bias. Further, there are only ten women partners in the firm, which strengthens our claim." There were only two female equity (ownership) partners, all the female litigation partners were part-time (by choice), and only one of the female equity partners had children. All female associates recently in corporate litigation had left the firm before partnership consideration. Attrition in the firm overall was high, and the vast majority of those leaving were female. All these conditions suggested to Margot a male-dominated power structure in the firm, which might easily result in biased treatment of female associates.

Meghan reviewed some of the additional evidence of discrimination. The senior partner who chaired the Associates Committee had stated that he had rated her low on "client satisfaction," despite high ratings in this area in her portfolio. The chair provided no specific facts in support of his rating, stating only that his opinion was that she was a prima donna. She was criticized by another senior partner for weak legal analysis skills, yet her overall rating in this area was the same as some of the male associates with whom she had been compared. In the Associates Committee's review, Ms. Evans was also criticized for being "too involved with women's issues in the firm" and "very demanding" and "insufficiently 'nonassertive and acquiescent'" to the predominantly male partnership. These comments suggested that she might have been punished in her review for raising issues in the firm or for not conforming to a submissive image or style.

At the time the Associates Committee at Wilson, Barnes declined to recommend Ms. Evans for partner, it did see fit to recommend a number of other associates. Out of a total of eight candidates in her class, five male associates and one female associate were recommended for regular partnership. One male associate was not recommended for either regular or special partnership. (As was commonly done, this associate would be offered a large cash settlement as part of his termination, but in exchange would have to file a release from any future legal action against the firm relating to its decision.) The evaluation portfolio data on the male associates most likely indicated that a few received higher ratings than Ms. Evans. The majority of the men recommended for partner were not superior to her, however, according to one committee member's analysis. The quantitative measures of associate success—including total hours billed, volume of business generated, and clients individually attracted to the firm—presented a picture of Ms. Evans's performance as equal to that of most of the men and superior to that of some who were recommended for partner. In addition, Ms. Evans had actually tried several cases, which was unusual for an associate in litigation, since many cases are settled without trial and the few that go to trial are usually handled by partners. The volume of business generated by Ms. Evans had steadily increased in the several years just before her review for partner, and her colleagues in the litigation department remarked on this as an indicator of her likely future productivity for the firm.

Meghan's legal case could also make the argument that several male associates were made partner despite scathing reviews in their portfolios; the cited failings of these associates were not used to block their recommendation for partnerships. A number were made partners despite serious concerns about general competence and behavior. One male associate was even deemed by the partners to have been guilty of malpractice (his guilt was in fact later established, after he left the firm) and yet was recommended for partner by the Executive Committee. The committee went so far as to excuse another male associate's frequent, lengthy, and unexplained absences (which created liabilities for the firm as a result of missed deadlines) because of his abilities in another area. Ms. Evans maintained that these recommendations were in stark contrast with her own evaluation, in which criticism of her analytical abilities—about which partners disagreed, and for which her overall rating in the last year was more than satisfactory—was given so much emphasis in the final evaluation. She believed that this criticism was unfairly used to negate her entire track record of accomplishment in the firm in other areas of the evaluation. Indeed, Evans was convinced she had met and in many ways exceeded the explicit standards the firm had set, and that she evidenced none of the serious character flaws manifested by more than one male associate accepted for partner. She had taken one year longer to achieve the hours required for partnership consideration, a consequence of a family leave, but the firm's policy allowed this.

This, then, would be the basis of Meghan's lawsuit, if she chose to file one. She would claim both that the firm's stated reason for considering her for partner—lack of legal analysis skill—was a cover for gender discrimination and that she had been treated differently from male colleagues. Written reviews of men who had made partner the same year Evans was denied would be read into the testimony in the case.

(Some of these were potentially very embarrassing to the firm; one man had been guilty of malpractice and another had disappeared without notice and missed critical deadlines.)

"It is a classic glass ceiling case," her attorney Margot argued, "denying a woman advancement to the highest levels of the professions and management on the basis of sex, while making up other reasons." She also argued that overall data about the firm—including fewer women associates staying long enough to seek partnership, fewer women with full access to the social networks that assisted in achieving partnership, reduction in volume of work following maternity and other family leaves taken, among other considerations—contributed to a male-dominated work culture generally in the firm.

The Firm's Likely Position

The firm of Wilson, Barnes, however, would undoubtedly make strong arguments of its own that it was not guilty of glass ceiling discrimination in denying Meghan a recommendation for partnership. The evaluation process allows for many interpretations, as there are no absolutely objective standards for judging performance. Some of the early evaluations of Meghan's legal analytical ability had been quite critical, from her early years with the firm, and the same issues arose in her final Associates Committee reviews. The firm would claim Meghan did not meet a minimum standard in legal analysis.

To the argument that Ms. Evans's other positive evaluations should have been allowed to offset some limitations in legal analysis, the firm was likely to cite a federal appeals court that had found that the final judgment of a legal firm should prevail in this matter. Their basic reasoning was that courts owe partnerships "special deference" in their decisions about conditions of employment. This line of argument presumes that small business associations ought not to be dictated by law but retain much latitude of judgment about selecting members and partners who fit the organization. This is an application of the freedom of association doctrine to small firms and groups. Of course, this position also reinforces whatever organizational culture prevails in the organization, by emphasizing that new leaders share the values and ethos of the incumbent group (*Ezold v. Wolf*, 1992).

In the same case, the court argued that it is not the job of the court to substitute its judgment about employment for that of the employer himself. The decision stated that the proper analysis should not have been whether in the court's view the lack of a particular legal ability was crucial to success as a partner. Rather, the court should analyze whether male associates who were granted partnership had been similarly criticized. The opinion of the court in this case stated that "the district court's comparison of plaintiff with successful male candidates in categories *other than* the specific legal ability in question" was not an appropriate role for the court to take.

Thus a court might decide that the evidence of a "hostile" environment toward women at Wilson, Barnes was not convincing. The attorney who had made "offensive" remarks to women had left the firm before Ms. Evans's partnership decision was made, he had been reprimanded, and he had been unlikely to make partner in any event. The court might also find that the small number of women partners in the firm did not, in itself, prove discrimination against women or that the evidence of discrimination in the assignments Ms. Evans was given was not sufficient to prove such discrimination on the basis of sex. Recently a male partner had argued, in a discussion of female attrition at the firm, that the firm was not responsible. "These young women often leave without applying for part-time work status, and without seeking adjustments. They are making lifestyle choices, and the firm is not responsible for those," he said.

Should Meghan Sue?

Margot, with her strength in employment law, continued to urge Meghan Evans to file a sex discrimination case in federal court. (A discrimination charge filed with the Equal Employment Opportunity Commission would have to precede the filing of a lawsuit; see Appendix C.) Margot believed the committee's recommendation was "a hideous injustice," and that the courts should prevent private firms such as Wilson, Barnes from using their freedom to exercise business judgment as a cover for prejudice and unlawful, unconstitutional discrimination in their employment practices. Seeing the Evans case as symbolic of the glass ceiling operating against the promotion of women and minorities to the highest and most lucrative positions in U.S. professions and businesses, Margot argued that she knew more than 60 groups that might offer to file amicus curiae ("friend of the court") briefs in support of Ms. Evans's case, if she brought one. Women's and civil-rights groups, in particular, were likely to come forward with support.

Meghan knew she had other options as well. She could file a discrimination complaint with the Equal Employment Opportunity Commission (EEOC) *without* subsequently bringing a lawsuit. Or she could simply resign for a different professional opportunity. She might with her substantial firm experience be able to move laterally to another major firm. This, however, could put her back into the same sort of dilemmas she had experienced at Wilson, Barnes. She could seek employment in a smaller firm, which might offer better working terms, but then again might not; she would have to be very cautious in her interviewing and raise the issues that had troubled her previously. She might start a small firm of her own, in conjunction with other attorneys seeking a more flexible work environment; this option of course involved considerable financial adjustment and risk. Finally, she could consider work in the public or nonprofit sector, which might involve less extreme work hours, but it would also result in a substantial financial cut.

"I just don't know what to do," she said again to Margot. "Maybe a challenging legal career is just beyond me right now."

❖ RELATED READINGS

American Bar Association. (2000). *Career satisfaction survey.* Chicago: Author.

American Bar Association. (2001). *Balanced lives: Changing the culture of legal practice.* Chicago: Author.

Epstein, C. F., Saute, R., Oglensky, B., & Gever, M. (1995). Glass ceilings and open doors: Women's advancement in the legal profession. *Fordham Law Review, 64,* 302–305.

Epstein, P. H. (2004). *Women-at-law: Lessons learned along the pathways to success.* Chicago: American Bar Association.

Ezold v. Wolf, Block, Schorr and Solis-Cohen, 983 F. 2d 509 (3rd Cir. 1992).

Glass Ceiling Commission. (1995). *A solid investment: Making full use of the nation's human capital.* Washington, DC: Government Printing Office.

Hull, R., & Nelson, R. K. (2000). Assimilation, choice, or constraint? Testing theories of gender differences in the careers of lawyers. *Social Forces, 79,* 229–264.

Karsten, M. F. (1994). Equal employment. In M. F. Karsten (Ed.), *Management and gender* (pp. 39–56). Westport, CT: Praeger.

Kay, F. M. (1997). Flight from law: A competing risks model of departures from law firms. *Law and Society Review, 31,* 301–335.

National Association for Legal Practice. (2003). *Keeping the keepers II: The management of associates.* Washington, DC: Author.

National Association of Women Lawyers. (1996, February 2). *The shoemaker's children—employment law issues relating to women and families in the law firm: A dialogue reflecting the firm's perspective and the lawyer's perspective.* NAWL Program at the American Bar Association Midwinter Meeting.

Noonan, M. C., & Corcoran, M. E. (2004, November). The mommy track and partnership: Temporary delay or dead end? *Annals of the American Academy of Political and Social Science, 596,* 130–150.

Nossel, S., & Westfall, E. (1998). *Presumed equal: What America's top women lawyers really think about their firms* (2d ed.). Franklin Lakes, NJ: Career Press.

Reichman, N. J., & Sterling, J. S. (2002). Recasting the brass ring: Deconstructing and reconstructing workplace opportunities for women lawyers. *Capital University Law Review, 29,* 923–977.

Rhode, Deborah. (2001). *The unfinished agenda: Women in the legal profession.* Chicago: American Bar Association Commission on Women in the Profession.

U.S. Equal Employment Opportunity Commission. (2003). *Diversity in law firms.* Retrieved August 28, 2006, at: www.eeoc.gov/stats/reports/diversity law/index.html

❖ STUDENT RESPONSE

1. What is the glass ceiling? How might it be relevant to Ms. Evans's case? Review the material in Appendix B on the glass ceiling.

2. What suggestions are there in the case that *informal norms* at Wilson, Barnes might have hurt Ms. Evans's case for partnership? Consider details in the case and the evaluations in Appendix A. What might these norms reveal about the organizational culture and values within the firm?

3. Why would Ms. Evans bother to sue Wilson, Barnes? Would an EEOC complaint *not* followed by a lawsuit, as described in Appendix C, be a better option? Why or why not?

4. How might James be a victim of sex discrimination?

5. Evaluate the likely arguments the firm could make, in defense of its decision about Meghan.

6. What would be the various costs to the firm of Wilson, Barnes if Meghan files a lawsuit against them?

7. Role plays or essay (one or more of these may be assigned by your instructor): Assume you are the following individual and describe (or act out) what actions you would take in the incident described in the case.

   – Ms. Evans's supervising partner, a supporter of her partnership
   – The employment attorney (Margot) consulted by Ms. Evans when she first learned she was denied partnership

- A female senior partner, not on the Associates or Executive Committee, who supports Evans
- A young female attorney entering Wilson, Barnes as a new associate
- A female attorney two years away from a partnership decision in Wilson, Barnes

Debate: Simulate a meeting of the Executive Committee in Wilson, Barnes, in which the arguments for and against granting partnership are debated.

8. Change agent: Develop a list of recommendations to the partners of Wilson, Barnes for improving the opportunity structure for women in the firm.

9. Develop a list of recommendations for improving the firm's evaluation process, on the basis of the guidelines presented in Appendix D.

APPENDIX A: SUMMARY OF MEGHAN EVANS'S EVALUATIONS OF LEGAL ANALYSIS

6th-Year Evaluations

Partner Name	Grade (Legal Analysis)	Comments
Promin	M	"I had minimal contact with Meghan, but I thought she did not generate ideas . . . or pull the facts together well and exercise the best lawyerly judgment. She seemed somewhat over her head, but I don't think she should have been." Recommended partnership with "negative feelings."
Kurt		"There seems to be serious question as to whether she has the legal ability to take on large matters and handle them on her own. We have been over this many times and there is nothing I can add to what I have already said about Meghan. What I envisioned about her when I hired her as a 'good, stand-up effective courtroom lawyer' remains true and I think she has proven her case. Apparently she has not proved to the satisfaction of the firm the other qualities considered necessary to rise to the top of the firm." Recommended partnership "with mixed emotions."
Alder	A	Slight contact. Recommended partnership "with mixed emotions."
Booke	A	"Meghan has avoided work requiring legal analysis ability because I believe she lacks it. On the other hand, in her case, other qualities redeem her. . . . I would not want her in charge of a large legally complex case, the traditional measure of a Wilson, Barnes partner." Recommended partnership "with favor."
Flahan	A	Slight contact. Recommended partnership with "mixed emotions."
Jones		"I have been singularly unimpressed with the level of her ability. . . . She may be fine to keep for certain smaller matters, but I don't see her skills as being those for our sophisticated

practice." Recommended partnership with "negative feelings."

Smith	G	"She is excellent in court and loves to be in that arena. She remains a little weak in her initial analysis of complex legal issues." Recommended partnership with favor.
Dubrin	A	"In my one experience we lost a client, but I think Meghan performed satisfactorily." No opinion on partnership admission.
Robins	G	Slight contact. Recommended partnership "with favor."
Spinaker	G	"Little contact, most favorable impression." Recommended partnership "with favor."

This summary focuses only on Meghan's grades in legal analysis, since that was the firm's reason for denial of her partnership. The above is a sampling of the Associates Committee's evaluation in this area and does not include all comments.

7th-Year Evaluations

Partner Name	Grade (Legal Analysis)	Comments
Rosen	A	"On a very complicated matter primarily involving financial analysis, I am not sure whether (she) grasped analysis fully. (I am not sure that others working on project did, either.) Recommended partnership with "mixed emotions."
Tomas	A	Slight contact. Recommended partnership "with mixed emotions."
Davins	A	"She will never be a legal scholar, but we have plenty of support in that area." Recommended partnership "with enthusiasm."
Arbit	A	"Barely adequate legal skills. Her abilities are limited. She makes a good impression but she lacks real legal analytical ability." Recommended partnership with "mixed emotions."
Fiedler	M	"Meghan has certain strengths. . . . If directed, she will do a good job, except that she has

		limitations with respect to complex legal issues. However, when left on her own she does not do what has to be done until (the) case is in crisis and she does a poor job in keeping (the) client informed." Recommended partnership with "negative feelings."
Goldberg	M	Would feel comfortable turning over a significant matter for one of my clients if not too complex. . . . Meghan reputedly can handle many of our matters on her own. If so and reliable others bear these rumors out, partnership may be in the cards." Recommended partnership with "negative feelings."
Jones	M	"Her abilities to grasp legal issues from the little I observed were insufficient to trust her in major litigation on her own." Recommended partnership with "negative feelings."
Pole	G	Slight contact. Recommended partnership "with favor."
Simmons	M	"Probably ancient history—but I do recall my perception that she does not write well and lacks intellectual sophistication." Recommended partnership with "negative feelings."
Fallows	G	"Meghan handled a moderate-sized lawsuit for a client of mine. Job was done well and responsibly. Result was good."
Robins	G	Slight contact; recommended partnership with "mixed emotions."
Gerb		"Experience with her years ago was unsatisfactory." No opinion on partnership.
Berman	G	Slight contact; recommended partnership "with enthusiasm."

In the sixth year, 91 partners submitted evaluations of Evans. Thirty-two, slightly over one-third, made recommendations, with varying degrees of confidence, for her admission to partnership. Seven of those recommended that she be made partner "with enthusiasm," 14 "with favor," 6 with "mixed emotions, 4 with "negative feelings," and 1 with "mixed emotions/negative feelings." After reviewing the evaluations and conducting interviews, the Associates Committee voted 9 to 1 not to recommend Evans for full partnership.

APPENDIX B: RECOMMENDATIONS OF
THE GLASS CEILING COMMISSION

Created as part of the Civil Rights Act of 1991, the 21-member bipartisan Glass Ceiling Commission was established to study and recommend ways to eliminate the barriers minorities and women experience when trying to advance into management and decision-making positions in the private sector. Members were appointed by the president and congressional leaders, and the commission was chaired by the secretary of labor. It focused on barriers and opportunities in three areas: (1) the filling of management and decision-making positions, (2) developmental and skill enhancing activities, and (3) compensation and reward activities. The commission prepared an extensive report on the glass ceiling entitled *A Solid Investment: Making Full Use of the Nation's Human Capital* (1995). In its final act, the commission adopted the following twelve recommendations for business and government to use in eliminating barriers that keep minorities and women out of the top management levels.

The recommendations to businesses and private firms were

1. Demonstrate CEO commitment.

2. Include diversity in all strategic business plans and hold line managers accountable for progress.

3. Use affirmative action as a tool.

4. Select, promote, and retain qualified individuals.

5. Prepare minorities and women for senior positions.

6. Educate corporate ranks.

7. Initiate work-life and family-friendly policies within firms.

8. Adopt high-performance workplace practices.

The recommendations to government were

1. Lead by example.

2. Strengthen enforcement of antidiscrimination laws.

3. Improve data collection.

4. Increase disclosure of diversity data.

APPENDIX C: U.S. EQUAL EMPLOYMENT OPPORTUNITY COMMISSION—INSTRUCTIONS FOR FILING A CHARGE

If you believe you have been discriminated against by an employer, labor union, or employment agency when applying for a job or while on the job because of your race, color, sex, religion, national origin, age, or disability, or believe that you have been discriminated against because of opposing a prohibited practice or participating in an equal employment opportunity matter, you may file a charge of discrimination with the U.S. Equal Employment Opportunity Commission (EEOC).

Charges may be filed in person, by mail, or by telephone by *contacting the nearest EEOC office*. If there is not an EEOC office in the immediate area, call toll free 800-669-4000 for more information. To avoid delay, call or write beforehand if you need special assistance, such as an interpreter, to file a charge.

There are strict time frames in which charges of employment discrimination must be filed. To preserve the ability of EEOC to act on your behalf and to protect your right to file a private lawsuit, should you ultimately need to, adhere to the following guidelines when filing a charge.

Title VII of the Civil Rights Act

Title VII charges must be filed with the EEOC within 180 days of the alleged discriminatory act. However, in states or localities where there is an antidiscrimination law and an agency authorized to grant or seek relief, a charge must be presented to that state or local agency. Furthermore, in such jurisdictions, you may file charges with the EEOC within 300 days of the discriminatory act, or 30 days after receiving notice that the state or local agency has terminated its processing of the charge, whichever is earlier. It is best to contact the EEOC promptly when discrimination is suspected. When charges or complaints are filed beyond these time frames, you may not be able to obtain any remedy.

SOURCE: Equal Opportunity Commission, Online. Retrieved August 25, 2006, at: www.eeoc.gov/charge/overview_charge_filing.html.

APPENDIX D: GUIDELINES FOR
EVALUATION OF LAW FIRM ASSOCIATES

Partners should recognize that the value of an associate's services and contribution to the firm cannot be determined with mathematical certainty nor can their overall performance be measured or described in terms of yards or meters, or any other precise unit of measure. . . . Partners also should recognize that rarely will an associate achieve the highest level in every established criterion. High marks in every category are not an absolute requirement for promotion to partner status. Nevertheless, the criteria, when considered as a whole, provide a law firm with a framework of discussion or at least some objective measure of comparison so that some degree of uniformity and fairness can be achieved in the process. The criteria are not listed in any priority; however, some carry more weight than others in particular firms.

Client Organization: Ability to develop and originate new clients.

Economic Consideration: A law firm must be able to justify the progression to partner on an economic basis. Economic factors may include (a) whether the practice area can sustain another partner; (b) the historical productivity (billable hours history); (c) the individual's ability to sustain high productivity at a partner's billing rate.

Longevity: Firms must set a minimum number of years before partnership consideration (commonly 6 to 8 years), but the amount of time varies from firm to firm.

Collection of Hours Billed

Client Relations

Handle Complex Matters with Minimal Supervision

Professional Skills: Associates must have demonstrated professional relations with clients and skills in legal analysis, writing, oral communications, and negotiating ability.

Case Management

Cooperative Spirit

Community Involvement

Personal Presentation

Nonbillable Hours: nonbillable time indicates commitment to the success of the firm.

SOURCE: Joel A. Rose. (2002, October 10). Criteria for making leap from associate to partner in firm management. *Business of Law, 227*(2), p. 5.

4

Medical Mentoring

CASE OVERVIEW

The primary subject of this case is the professional development of women and the potential value of mentoring in that process. A meeting of women physicians provides the setting. Women in medical school and at the initial stages of their careers share with more established women doctors a discussion of the current professional situation of women in medicine, including general practice, highly specialized subfields, and academic medicine. The discussion ranges over a variety of problems encountered, with supporting data for the major points. Income, work demands, specialties, advancement in academic medicine, and places of employment all appear different for male and female physicians. The case requires a minimal background in organizational culture and professional advancement issues.

❖ BODY OF CASE

The 40 or so women milled around the conference room until the chair, Ellen Davis, called the session to order. "We are happy, tonight, to have as our invited guests a number of young women who are enrolled in the Orchard University School of Medicine, as well as a number of new practitioners and medical school faculty members. Our chapter of American Medical Women is delighted that you are here. We seek to involve you in our organization, which attempts to serve the special needs of women doctors in our area. Tonight we are especially interested in what problems or concerns you are facing or worries you have. We hope to develop some activities or programs designed especially to address these concerns as a result of tonight's session. To help focus our discussion, a panel, representing various medical specialties and positions, has done some initial research on the current experiences of women in their fields. They will each share some findings with us. This will give us a starting point, after which we hope everyone will chime in with information and suggestions for specific actions we might take here in our own chapter.

Let me first introduce the panel:

Linda Rodriguez is a fourth-year medical student at Orchard U., and she will share some information about the experiences of female medical students.

Marcia Birthright has been in family practice with several other physicians for 10 years and is also raising a family of her own.

Amelia Pioneer is an otolaryngologist [a specialist in head and neck surgery] and is also on the surgical faculty of Orchard U. Medical School.

Nancy Jenner is a specialist in pediatrics and also serves as chair of the regional chapter of the American Medical Association.

We welcome each of you panelists and appreciate the work you have done preparing for tonight's meeting. Linda, let's start with you; what are some of the current issues about women in medical school?"

"Well, Ellen, there is good news and bad news. On the one hand, more women than ever are applying to and being accepted in medical school. There is concern that many young girls are still not encouraged to excel in mathematics and science, especially between the ages of 11 and 15. However, women constituted 47.9% of the student body in medical schools in 2003, in contrast to less than 10% in the 1960s and 1970s, and women represented 40% of all medical residents in 2001 compared to 21.5% in 1980 (American Medical Association [AMA], 2004). About 45% of the students at the Orchard University Medical School are currently women. The increases in female medical students are, of course, related to the quadrupling of women in the profession overall during the past 20 years. As most of you probably know, women represented 25.8% of all U.S. physicians in 2003, and some have predicted that by the year 2010, 30% of U.S. physicians will be women.

Many female students in Orchard Med feel that, while accepted on the surface, they are not given the same quality of attention and sponsorship that male medical students receive. Furthermore, some of us believe that we are being steered toward certain 'female' specialties and residencies. Both students and faculty seem to have preconceived notions about who fits into which specialty, and some of the notions seem to relate to gender. The fields most commonly recommended for women are pediatrics, psychiatry, and anesthesiology. Female students feel these fields have an advantage in that women are already well accepted into them. However, it seems that a number of women feel less free to follow their true preferences for their specialty than men feel. Obtaining sponsorship in the fields less populated by women is definitely difficult for many of us.

We have formed an association of women medical students and hope to provide some mutual support through that group. In this student group, we are developing a newsletter to share our personal experiences, inviting prominent women physicians to speak to us on various topics, sponsoring an annual retreat, joining with women medical students elsewhere in the country, and exploring connections with the American Medical Women's Association. We are here tonight also because we hope that this group, with all your experience, may be helpful to us. We are looking forward to hearing what the other members of the panel and the group as a whole have to say about women's current experiences in medicine."

"Thank you, Linda. Your remark about being urged to consider some specialties more than others may relate to some of the research Amelia and Nancy have done, about the current status of women in the various specialties. Amelia, as a highly specialized surgeon, how would you respond to Linda's observations?"

"Well, of course, I am on the medical school faculty myself, so I certainly hope that would be one contact point for Linda and her peers, if they are interested in otolaryngology or other surgical specialties. I do remember in my own med school years, however, that we women were not encouraged to pursue surgery in particular, because it was so competitive. The men felt they would make better use of the internships and residencies than women, who might interrupt their careers for family. I know we will return to discuss some family issues, later.

As to specialties, it is clear in data I obtained from the AMA that women more than men concentrate, in rank order, in internal medicine, pediatrics, family practice, obstetrics/gynecology, psychiatry, and anesthesiology; these specialties accounted for 62.6% of all female physicians in 2003. Further, that list has been about the same since the early 1990s. Most women also practice in primary care situations, dealing directly with patients; 84% of female physicians in 2003 were in patient care and 68.9% were in office-based practice. In contrast, surgery ranked third in the choices of male physicians, and tenth among females. Women are still relatively rare in the highly prestigious areas of radiology, surgery, and cardiology.

Very few women choose surgery, which is reflected in my specialty. By 1996 the American College of Surgeons reported that only 24.4% of those completing surgical residencies were female, despite the increasing number of female medical students. Also, in academia, women are less apt to advance and receive high salaries than are men.

I know that some women doctors believe that women enter the primary care fields of their own volition, because they prefer them for a variety of reasons. Others have argued, however, that women are forced into these areas of medicine. Dr. Lila A. Wallis, a past president of the American Medical Women's Association, recently stated that 'Women have been pushed into primary care. They aren't always encouraged to go into the high-tech specialties.' This sounds more like the experience Linda and some of her colleagues seem to be having at Orchard.

Some research has suggested that women are particularly good at providing primary care. A study of medical students in Arizona in the 1980s indicated that medical students found women physicians to be 'more sensitive, more altruistic, and less egoistic.' So perhaps women do seek out these positions because they are well suited for them. On the other hand, I am not convinced that the great discrepancies between the numbers of men and of women are primarily due to differences in aptitudes. I suspect there are still barriers operating here.

In my own field of otolaryngological surgery, there are other differences between men and women, besides just their numbers in the practice. Only 4.1% of female physicians were in the fields of medical teaching, administration, and research. While there are no real differences in background, more men than women are in university practices, which tend to be more visible and prestigious. Only 22.8% of medical faculty members are female. Within universities, there are very different salaries and almost twice as many men are full professors. Women feel that promotion practices are often unfair, and men are unlikely to encourage women to pursue this career path. Some of these findings were from a recent survey of surgeons themselves. They certainly confirm the experience with the competitive specialties and recruiting for them that Linda and her peers have at Orchard.

In academic medicine as a whole, not just surgery, women do far less well than men. I already mentioned differences at the rank of full professor. In 1992 less than 3% of the medical schools were administered by women, and women are less likely than men to move into tenure-track positions in medical schools. Only 24% of the full-time medical school faculty members in 1994 were women; by 2003 the percentage of women was about 30% of all medical faculty. By 2003, 10% of all medical school department chairs, and 10% of all medical school deans, were female—still a small number given the number of women in the profession. (If these women do not advance, we will truly have evidence of a 'glass ceiling' in academic medicine.) Several studies early in the new century suggested salary discrimination in academic medicine, even when factors such as experience and working hours were controlled."

Ellen turned to Nancy, the pediatric specialist on the panel. "Nancy, how do you feel about these differences in numbers of men and women in the various fields, and what have you encountered along these lines in your own career?"

"Well, Ellen, I'd certainly like to believe I chose pediatrics freely, not because it is a 'woman's field.' Pediatrics is an office-based field, of course, and between 1970 and 1990 women physicians in patient care increased by more than 100%, which was largely explained by the increase in women physicians in office-based practice. As of 2003, 68.9% of women doctors are office-based, which is higher than the number of men, who are more apt to be hospital-based. Marcia, who is also in an office-based practice, may also want to comment on this when she speaks.

I have an additional concern, however, in my role as chair of the Orchard chapter of the AMA," Nancy continued. "Women have just not achieved leadership positions in our professional groups in numbers that are commensurate with our representation in medicine. Over the years, women physicians have also been less likely to join medical societies such as the AMA, although the American Medical Women's Association, of which we are a part tonight, has a proud tradition.

As in academic medicine, there is some evidence that women are now beginning to emerge as leaders in professional organizations. The number of women in the House of Delegates of the AMA has increased from 5% in 1989 to 10% in 1994 and has continued to rise since then. Recently, in fact, the first women chair of the AMA board of trustees, Nancy Dickey, served with distinction. One third of the presidents of state and county medical specialty societies, and 59% of the members of national societies, are women. So progress in this area seems steady, if slow.

A summit of women leaders in medicine was convened to assess the needs of women doctors, and they cited leadership development as a priority. Perhaps we can discuss some of their other recommendations later, when we get around to talking about action."

"Thank you, Nancy," Ellen said. "I think before opening things up, we should now hear from Marcia Birthright, who is in her tenth year of family practice here in the area. Marcia, what issues do you feel we haven't touched on yet?"

"My concerns, Ellen, have to do with some of the reasons behind the data we have been discussing. I agree with Nancy, that many of us choose office-based and primary care positions freely and because of our aptitudes for these practices. Most women physicians are married, half of them to male physicians, and a great majority have children, as I do. I suspect, then, that many women choose office-based work because of its more flexible hours. In 2005 the Women Physicians Congress reported that women physicians averaged 49 hours of work per week, compared to the men's average of 57 hours, suggesting that women physicians hold more time in reserve for family concerns. Women also spend more time with each patient. The AMA says that female physicians schedule fewer patients per hour and per week than do their male counterparts.

"Women are about twice as likely as men to be employed by a hospital, HMO, group practice, or other organization. Forty-three percent of women doctors are employees, compared with 22% of men. Just 57% of women doctors work alone, with a partner, as part owner in a group practice, or as an independent contractor. For men doctors, the proportion is 79%. While independent practitioners generally earn more money, they also tend to work longer hours and must contend with more paperwork and other administrative duties.

We haven't really discussed earnings much, but of course we all know women doctors earn much less than men, for a variety of reasons we have mentioned: They are concentrated in less lucrative specialties; they tend to work fewer hours; they are not as advanced, in academic rank. In 1992, the net average earnings of women averaged 62% of the net earned by men in 1992, according to the AMA. Even among women in practice for twenty or more years, the earnings were 72% of those of men. According to the 2000 census, this has not changed; women doctors by 1999 were making 62% of what male doctors earned.

"I, myself, am in the midst of juggling my career with high family demands. I have a husband whom I love very much and who loves me very much, and we're very committed to our children and to each other, as well as to our careers. I work a four-day week, which adds up to 40 to 50 hours per week. My husband and I share grocery shopping, errands, and cooking. We hire some household help and also have excellent caretakers for the kids. On weekends, when I'm not on call, I'm really with the kids all the time.

"I think this balance would be harder to maintain were I not in practice with another woman physician. We understand each other's needs, and we understand how important family is. I think we are typical of many women physicians, who have looked for career opportunities that give us more flexibility. The financial aspects are not super important to me. However, I do bristle when my work or career is compared to those of men. As long as you judge me on the basis of hours worked, rather than what I produce, there's no way, as a working mother, I can compete. And I wouldn't say I have the solutions, yet, to the problems of working parents. I often feel I am sort of two-timing everyone in my life. I'm still struggling."

Nancy the surgeon chimed in at this point. "That's true for all women physicians, maybe all women professionals. We are being asked to accommodate to the rules that were set up for the 1960s male. We are breaking new ground, still. We hope when we choose a field to enter we may do so according to what we find more interesting and that we are not hampered in that decision by questions of male dominance, glass ceilings, and restricted promotions. I think it is also imperative that women, who are doing somewhat better in medical-practice settings, achieve greater prominence in academic and organized medicine as well."

Ellen turned her attention to the entire group. "I wonder if some of our younger guests would care to respond to any of these informative reports. Do you find yourself troubled or encouraged by what you have heard?"

One of the medical students stirred and began to speak. "I think most of us still in training recognize the reality of the pictures that have been painted here, of the pressures toward primary care and the hesitancy to pursue the more competitive specialties, even if those are the most appealing. I feel drawn toward radiology, yet the faculty in that area are not particularly encouraging, and I don't know whom to talk to about my choices, obstacles I might run into, and so on. How can we feel less lonely and also be professionally realistic in our career assessments and decisions? When I talk to my male colleagues, they just don't seem to feel these dilemmas in quite the same way."

Marcia Jenner responded eagerly. "The summit of women medical leaders I mentioned earlier agreed with the importance of just those concerns. Those women doctors at the summit recognized the need for support for women physicians; they called for formal structures to provide more effective and consistent, uniform mentoring of women in medicine. Women face the challenge of achieving balance between the overlapping demands of career and personal responsibilities, often more than men do, as we've heard here tonight.

We all recognize the importance of sponsorship in establishing a successful medical career, and mentoring is an important aspect of that. Also, the summit leaders believed that elements of mentoring and mentoring relationships are characteristically different for men than for women; it is often more difficult for women to identify or approach potential mentors. Faculty members who have the potential to serve in this capacity are frequently too busy to assume the role.

The summit concluded that multiple strategies need to be developed to increase the number of mentors and to encourage women physicians to seek out mentoring relationships. The need for men as well as women to assume mentoring responsibilities was emphasized. I think the summit participants are really on to something important, and we should develop a mentoring program."

"I'm not so sure," responded another young doctor. "I have so much to juggle already, I'd hate to waste time just chatting with someone to no particular point."

"What do some of the rest of you think?" asked Ellen. "Is mentoring a possibility we should pursue?"

"We all know how important sponsorship is, early in our careers," responded another. "The acceptable novice physician becomes a sort of protégé of a member of the elite group of established physicians and thus gets referrals of patients, secures affiliation with the community's most prestigious hospitals, and is offered partnerships and other valuable connections. The initial sponsorship seems to make the new doctor visible to colleagues and gives her a chance to demonstrate competence. As we heard earlier, women are still not represented in some of the more elite inner circles of medicine, and perhaps lack of initial sponsorship or mentoring is one of the reasons."

"I think mentoring also would help us navigate the family-versus-profession difficulties that have been mentioned. It couldn't hurt to discuss those, especially with other women who've 'been there, done that,'" suggested another member.

"But does mentoring really achieve anything?" asked the initial skeptic. Ellen responded with some additional outside information. "Well, there is currently a national program, sponsored by the Women's Leadership Forum, designed to help 12 already successful women, mostly in business, work with mentors who are even *more* successful women, in the same fields. The program is building on the experience of the women who have already overcome barriers in their careers and have come forward to help mentor others. In this program the goal is to identify the obstacles facing the women who are attempting to develop the next stage of their careers. The mentor and protégé work to identify the obstacles, and the mentor shares suggestions for overcoming them. I think this model might work in medicine, too."

"I have a friend, also in business, in Minnesota, who is at an earlier stage in her career and is participating in a larger mentoring initiative," contributed another. "This program also was in response to the Glass-Ceiling Initiative. The program brings together 100 outstanding women with 100 business leaders in a year-long, one-on-one relationship. Half the mentors are men and half are women, all volunteers.

The basic requirements of this program include a leadership assessment of the protégé, including confidential interviews with her manager, peers, and subordinates, followed by a minimum of 14 hours of one-on-one counseling with the mentor; more time may be spent, but participants commit to the 14 hours. The program also provides eight days of training for the protégés and mentoring guidelines for the mentors, with the advice that mentors should use their own experience to guide their protégés. Some of the biggest companies in the Midwest are participating. Initial evaluation suggests this program is providing concrete help to the women involved, and a great many mentors have already indicated their willingness to sign on for another year. I like the clear definition this program seems to have."

One of the medical students seemed interested at this point. "In our Women Medical Students group we have wondered if there are enough women in the various fields of medicine for us to contact. With small numbers, it seems as if we may need to use a group mentoring approach, where one senior woman relates to a number of younger ones, yet I'm not sure that would be as effective. Or maybe we should follow the Minnesota approach, and use men as mentors also. That would mean less support on the personal issues, though. I'm not sure how I feel about this issue of recruiting the appropriate mentors, and who they are, in medicine."

"Do all the mentors and protégés necessarily have to be in the same location?" asked another student. "Maybe videoconferencing and e-mail or other technology could be used to connect mentors and protégés."

"I also think, later in careers, that a sort of peer-mentoring approach might be useful," said a woman who had been in practice for several years. "I think the connections need to be with women at similar stages of career advancement, as well as with those more senior. Peers are also good counselors, since they face similar obstacles."

"Medical students could also mentor undergraduates, and even girls in the community who are interested in science but short on encouragement and ideas," contributed another student.

"But what's in it for the mentor?" asked a well-established physician. "I think it is important to get our institutions and organizations, associations, hospitals, and so on, to recognize the importance of this activity. Several studies have shown that it is important to have unequivocal support of the mentoring concept from the senior management or whoever is important in the leadership of organizations. This gives the mentors encouragement to take the assignment seriously, and also allows the professional time needed to carry it out."

"Most of all," added another, "we would need to be very clear about the nature of the mentoring relationship, the responsibilities of both the mentor and the protégé, and the topics that would likely be addressed in the relationship. This lets everyone know what they are getting involved in, and also increases the probability of success, since expectations are clear from the beginning."

"It seems to me that we've accomplished a lot," said Ellen. "We have identified a lot of important issues facing us and other women in medicine. We have also, it seems, reached agreement that a mentoring program would be useful. I'd like to appoint a subcommittee to develop a suggested mentoring program for our chapter to consider. Please address the key issues about mentoring we've examined, plus any others you think are important. These would include the following:

- A description of the mentoring relationship and the potential benefits for both parties
- The specific responsibilities of both the mentor and the protégé, the expectations and limitations, especially as these relate to commitments of time
- The likely issues to be discussed or addressed in the mentoring relationships, in light of the problems we discussed earlier tonight
- Identification and recruitment of mentors

- Organizational issues, sponsorship, and support for the program
- How, when, and by whom the mentoring program should be evaluated

"Thank you all very much for coming, and we will look forward to the subcommittee's report."

❖ RELATED READINGS

Albaugh, G. K., Bellavance, E., Hadeed, J. H., Parker, M., & Alexander, J. B. (2003, October). Gender specific differences influencing choice of specialty and opinion of surgery among medical students. *Journal of Surgical Research, 114*(2), 296.

American College of Surgeons. (2000). Results: 1994–1995 and 1995–1996 graduates of surgical residencies. Retrieved August 25, 2006, at: www.facs.org/jacs/lead_articles/jun99results.html

American Medical Association. (1994). *Report on the women physician leaders' summit*. Chicago: Author.

American Medical Association. (2000). *Physician masterfile, Dec. 2000*. Chicago: Author.

American Medical Association. (2003). *Characteristics of physicians, 2003*. Chicago: Author.

American Medical Association. (2004). *Physician characteristics and distribution in the US, 2003–2004 edition*. Chicago: Author.

American Medical Association. (2005). *Characteristics of physicians, 2005*. Chicago: Author.

Association of American Medical Colleges. (2004). *Women in U.S. academic medicine: Statistics and medical school benchmarking, 2003–2004*. Retrieved August 26, 2006, at: www.aamc.org/members/wim/statistics/stats04/start.htm

Boulis, A. (2004, November). The evolution of gender and motherhood in contemporary medicine. *Annals of the American Academy of Political and Social Science, 596*, 172–181.

Braus, P. (1994). How women will change medicine. *American Demographics, 16*, 40–46.

Carr, P. L., Szalacha, L., Barnett, R., Caswell, C., & Inui, L. (2003, December). A ton of feathers: Gender discrimination in academic medical careers and how to manage it. *Journal of Women's Health, 12* (10), 1009–1018.

Croasdale, M. (2004, September). The 63% question: Why are female physicians lagging behind? *American Medical News*. Retrieved August 21, 2006, at: www.womensderm.org/news/63_percent_question.html

Eisenberg, C. (1989). Medicine is no longer a man's profession: Or, when the men's club goes coed, it's time to change the regs. *New England Journal of Medicine, 321*, 1542–1544.

Finley, M. (1995). *When the doctor is a woman, from women like us,* reprinted on the Internet home page of Women in Medicine, University of Texas at Austin.

Fong, K. M. (1995, November 19). Women mentoring women will overcome glass-ceiling barriers. *Los Angeles Times,* p. B2.

Fried, L. P., Francomano, C. A., MacDonald, S. M., Wagner, E. M., Stokes, E. J., Carbone, K. M., Bias, W. B., Newman, M. M., & Stobo, J. D. (1996). Career development for women in academic medicine: Multiple interventions in a department of medicine. *Journal of the American Medical Association, 276,* 898–905.

Higgins, L. (1994). Mentoring moves mountains. *Stanford Medicine, 11,* 4–8.

Komaromy, M., Bindman, A. B., Haber, R. J., & Sande, M. A. (1993). Sexual harassment in medical training. *New England Journal of Medicine, 328,* 322–326.

Levy, D. (1996, August 6). Women doctors see earnings picture improve. *USA Today.*

Lorber, J. (1984). *Women physicians.* New York: Tavistock.

Massachusetts Medical Society. (1996). Editorial: Women physicians—good news and bad news. *New England Journal of Medicine, 334,* 982–983.

Ragins, B. R. (1999). Gender and mentoring relationships: A review and research agenda for the next decade. In G. N. Powell (Ed.), *Handbook of gender and work* (pp. 347–370). Thousand Oaks, CA: Sage.

Robinson, G. E. (2004). Career satisfaction in female physicians. *Student Journal of American Medical Association, 291,* 635. Retrieved August 25, 2006, at: jama.ama.assn.org/cgi/content/full/291/5/635.

U.S. Census. (2000). Evidence from Census 2000 about earnings by detailed occupation for men and women. Retrieved August 20, 2006, at: www.census.gov/prod/2004pubs/censr-15.pdf

Women's Physicians Congress. (2005). Table 5: Women physicians by specialties. Retrieved May 20, 2006 at: www.ama-assn.org/ama/pub/category/12916.html

❖ STUDENT RESPONSE

1. Working in groups assigned by your instructor, develop a mentoring program for the Orchard chapter of the American Women's Association. Address the specific issues for female physicians raised by the chair at the conclusion of the meeting, being sure that your plan includes

   - a description of the mentoring relationship and the specific potential benefits for both parties
   - the specific responsibilities of both the mentor and the protégé and the expectations and limitations

   – the likely issues to be discussed or addressed in the mentor-
     ing relationships
   – how you would identify and recruit mentors
   – organizational issues, such as sponsorship and personal and
     financial support for the program
   – how, when, how often, and by whom the mentoring program
     should be evaluated

2. If you are in a classroom setting, develop a presentation of your
   plan for your class. Assume you are arguing for your plan to the
   chapter who appointed you to develop it. Your presentation
   should not exceed 15 minutes, since other proposals will also be
   made. Use appropriate supporting materials, such as handouts
   and charts, to summarize your major points.

3. Which of the problems faced by women physicians are best
   addressed by mentoring? Why?

4. Are there problems faced by women physicians that are not
   particularly well addressed by mentoring? Why?

5. In your mentoring plan, how do you recommend recruiting the
   mentors needed for these young women physicians? Do you
   anticipate any problems in recruitment? How will you "sell"
   the idea to prospective mentors who, in this case, are already
   very busy?

6. Having seen the issues and problems discussed in the case, do
   you recommend male as well as female mentors in your plan?
   Why or why not?

7. Do you think the idea of "group mentoring," suggested in the
   case, would work well in this situation? Why or why not?

8. Do you like the idea of "long distance" mentoring? Why or why
   not?

9. What are the specific ways of evaluating a mentoring program?
   In the discussion of evaluation in Item 1 above, what measur-
   able outcomes could be included?

5

The Pregnant Professor

❖ BODY OF CASE

"You'd be fools to marry," exclaimed the dean of Arts and Sciences to the two outstanding Ph.D. candidates in front of him. "Do you know how tight the academic job market is? You'll be lucky to find one permanent job, let alone two!"

The two young scholars, of course, did not heed this warning. Tim had finished all his work except the dissertation, and his new spouse, Karen, was just ready to begin her dissertation research. At that point the two entered the teaching job market in economics. Hoping to find tenure-track positions in the same location, they were sadly disappointed. Tim accepted a position in New York City, while Karen landed a position in the prestigious Midwest University.

"We were groomed," she later said, "in graduate school to take the 'best' position, in the most prestigious department. We assumed this would lead to better pay, working conditions, students, and all the rest. I guess I was pretty naïve not to ask more questions." Thus the couple began a three-year period of commuting between New York and the Midwest.

"I was wary of putting my career on hold to follow Tim," Karen explained, "because I had seen other couples start out a marriage with great intentions of equality, only to resort to traditional gender roles, obviously favoring the man's career, when real decisions had to be made." No definite limits were placed on the length of time they would commute, and they had no real plan for terminating the commuting arrangement.

"Both of us found our jobs more difficult than we had ever really imagined," Tim reported later. "I didn't much like teaching, and it took up so much time that I didn't finish my dissertation in the first year, as I'd planned." Karen did finish her dissertation during her first year at Midwest University, but felt she compromised its quality in yielding to departmental pressure to finish it and actively publish other work. Meanwhile, the commuting was hard on them both. "Having two stressful jobs without the daily support of the other person was a drag, and the expense was quite a problem," Karen admits.

After three years, Tim quit his eastern position and moved to the Midwest. Karen's university was in a state capital, and Tim obtained a position as a policy analyst in a government agency. About the same time, Karen discovered she was pregnant. She had wanted a child and had worried about delaying pregnancy because there were fertility problems in her family. But she also knew that a pregnancy would complicate her life in an academic department where professors "were supposed to work all the time and never have a life." She recalled being told by one of the tenured (permanent) faculty that if she had commitments outside the department she shouldn't tell anyone about it, as they would think that she wasn't serious about academia. Still, "I knew I wanted a child and I didn't want to take the risk of waiting until my career was on more solid ground—which it wasn't at the time—as it was taking me a while to get my research published."

As it turned out, Karen was informed, during the second trimester of her pregnancy, that her contract would not be renewed for the following year. The university had yearly contracts for its assistant professors (something she had not asked about when applying for her position). The previous year, the department had been quite critical of her, not the quality of her work, but the quantity and the speed with which she was getting things published. They decided during her fourth year that she surely would not achieve tenure in the sixth year, and so they would terminate her before the tenure decision point. (It was, she described, a "general bloodletting," for three assistant professors in her department were terminated.)

"I thought it was sleazy," she said as she shared with a friend, "since I was not told until the week I was notified my contract wouldn't be renewed that this was even a possibility. There were several ways to stop the tenure clock (which would allow more time before the tenure decision) if all they were worried about was the clock running out. First, anytime one went on unpaid leave the tenure clock could stop; when I interviewed, they made constant reference to this policy. So I could have been allowed to take unpaid leave. Second, the university was in the process of adopting a policy of stopping the tenure clock when an assistant professor had a baby, though the policy was not yet formally approved. But these policies were both ignored by my department and I was let go."

Karen realized she might have sued Midwest University, but she did not have the emotional energy to do so. She was also filled with self-doubt and questioned her own dedication to the academic life, even after a very successful career as an undergraduate and graduate student. So she "retreated" and accepted a part-time temporary position in state government, during which she hoped to redefine her career goals and strategies. Her decision and her new job occurred when her baby was about six months old.

Meanwhile, Tim was learning a lot in his own government position. He had mastered writing regulations and other forms of writing effectively, negotiating with many types of people, and working in a bureaucracy. He was, however, working about 60 hours a week, in addition to sharing care of the couple's infant daughter. He couldn't seem to get any writing done, and his dissertation languished as a result. He found himself open to the idea of another change in their goals as a couple.

Karen reported another problem with Tim's government job. "My husband's office was terrible about recognizing the demands of having a new baby. We came home from the hospital on Wednesday and one of Tim's coauthors wanted him to come to a meeting on Friday. When Friday rolled around, I just told Tim not to go, to say that he couldn't leave me alone. (This wasn't really true, but I'll lie when I have to.) He already had an important meeting scheduled, requiring lots of preparation on Sunday and Monday. It was a crazy time, and I'm not sure how he did it."

While finishing at the university and later working in her temporary job, Karen also was conducting research with a colleague at a small liberal arts college nearby. Karen observed that this colleague had more "people contact" and personal freedom than Karen experienced at Midwest University, and also she was energized by her contact with undergraduate students and colleagues in many academic disciplines.

"I had figured out that what stifled me at Midwest University was the lack of energy I got from other people, from my work environment itself. I was supposed to sit in my office, or the library, or my apartment, all day, doing research all by myself, and I just couldn't do it. It drove me nuts; I needed to get energy from the people and place around me. (Earlier when I had complained to the department chair about the lack of any intellectual exchange at Midwest, he said to me, 'Well, this is not a social club.') I also didn't like the narrowness of the research university, the concentration on our own narrow specialties to the exclusion of everything else. It was the connections between my work and the 'everything else' that made academic work interesting to me."

A mentor, a female colleague in another department at Midwest University was another influence on Karen during this transitional period. The news that female assistant professors were leaving the university at a higher rate than male assistant professors had provided the impetus to establishing a mentoring program for women professors.

Karen reports that "I was hooked up with a woman in another department who was absolutely fantastic. I requested someone with children, and she understood what was going on, so I didn't have to justify or defend myself. She also let me know that my department at Midwest didn't have to act the way they did, that other departments at the university would have made different decisions and offered me some alternatives when I was pregnant. She helped me revise my vita and told me I should feel comfortable applying for any job I wanted.

"I decided a liberal arts college might be better for me," Karen states. "I was somewhat in a panic, since I had nothing lined up. I felt like I was jumping into the great unknown. I worried about it, but it was also somewhat freeing. I didn't have to worry about what other people would think about me, or what they wanted me to do; I only had to figure out what I wanted."

Eventually Karen did look for a liberal arts faculty position. She reported that she was "picky" about choosing a desirable location, for herself and her family, as well as a college with a good reputation and working conditions.

"I was willing to stay in academia, but only on my own terms. I wasn't willing to settle for a mediocre school or position. On the other hand, in my temporary government job I had missed the intellectual life of academia—the supposing, and hypothesizing, and playing with ideas. So I went back on the academic job market."

The first year there were no positions that met Karen's criteria. The second year she was lucky, however: there were six liberal arts jobs in places acceptable to her and to Tim, and she was offered a desirable one. "Tim was very supportive," Karen recalls. "If we moved to Worth, he could spend some time finishing his dissertation. He also thought the job was a good one for me. He liked the idea of living in New England, where Worth was located. He was willing to move without _____ place. I, on the other hand, was wary and risk-averse. _____ out what would happen if I didn't like Worth, or _____ me. We'd be stuck out there, with no obvious way of _____ didn't want to spend five to seven years putting _____ place, only to have to move if I were denied tenure. _____ to it."

_____ of this move to Worth College, the couple's child was _____ they "bought as much child care as they could afford" so that _____ld work on completing his dissertation; he also did some part-time consulting for his previous employer in the Midwest, which eased his transition to their new location. Karen, meanwhile, started her tenure clock over at Worth, even though she had taught for four years, and published a book and a number of articles, which, she felt, "was enough to be an associate professor just about anyplace."

"I didn't mind starting the tenure process over, because it took the immediate pressure off. I considered myself 'mommy-tracked' even though no one ever said that to me, and I never told anyone else that that's what I was doing," Karen states. "I was slowing the progress to tenure, on purpose, to give myself more time before that critical decision came up again." She found the demands of teaching in a small college intense and time-consuming.

"To manage my time, I came up with several tricks, like slotting so much time for preparing for class and not spending any more time than that on preparation, or having a quota of papers to grade every day in order to get them done on time. But I think the most important decision I ever made was to live my life now, as opposed to waiting until I got tenure to have a life, and just accept the consequences. I would stay in academia on my terms."

She found Worth somewhat more hospitable to her terms. "Many of the faculty here have small children and expect to spend time with them," she said of the college. "I see little kids at work quite often, and no one blinks an eye when I show up with mine. Because it's a small college, far from a big city, I think it probably attracts people who want to have children and spend time with them. Midwest University was terrible on this score. We never heard about anybody having a life outside work, and certainly I didn't see children in the offices."

On both faculties, however, Karen found there are many extracurricular expectations of professors. "There are many after-hours meetings and dinners—work as socializing. I will do some of these, and refuse others—it depends on what is going on at home and how much I have been away recently."

Tim took a couple of years to finish his dissertation. Just as Karen was due to go on "assistant professor leave"—a year provided at half salary so assistant professors can take a full year's leave in their fourth year, prior to the tenure decision—Tim found a great job in a nearby state capital, as a research fellow at the Economics Institute, a private think tank. The institute was an hour's drive away from Worth, but Tim and Karen both report that, "since Worth is in the middle of nowhere," they feel pretty fortunate. It is common for spouses of Worth faculty not to find jobs. As Karen ironically points out, "This mostly applies to women, of course; it seems like when it's the man who can't find work, the couple moves away." And Tim adds that his new position was the kind of job he really wanted to have, one that eventually might take him back to state government, a possible future goal.

During Karen's assistant professor leave she started thinking about having another child. She was ambivalent, mainly because she hated being pregnant and being a pregnant assistant professor at Midwest University had drastically complicated her life. She spent a lot of time talking with other female faculty friends about when they should have children—would it hurt them if they got pregnant now or later, should they take maternity leave, who could they talk to about their decisions, and similar questions. They were aware of the small percentage of female full professors, nationally, who have children at all. It takes so long to finish the Ph.D., then six more years to earn tenure, so that by the time many women finish these first career stages, the best childbirth years are over.

Karen wrestled with her own questions. Should she wait until she came up for tenure to have another baby? She was already in her late thirties and waiting just made it more unlikely that she would get pregnant. But if she became pregnant while an untenured assistant professor, how would she manage? What would happen? Could she risk her job security a second time, after all she and Tim had already been through?

❖ RELATED READINGS

Blair-Loy, M. (2003). *Competing devotions: Career and family among women executives.* Cambridge, MA: Harvard University Press.

Feldman, C. (1997). *I work too: Working wives talk about their dual-career lives.* Santa Barbara, CA: Blue Point.

Gappa, J. M., & Leslie, D. (1993). *The invisible faculty: Improving the status of part-timers in higher education.* San Francisco: Jossey-Bass.

Hochschild, A. (1989). *The second shift.* New York: Viking.

Jacobs, J. (2004). The faculty time divide. *Sociological Forum, 19*(1), 3–27.

Jacobs, J., & Winslow, S. E. (2004). Overworked faculty: Job stresses and family demands. *Annals of the American Academy of Political and Social Science, 596,* 104–129.

Mason, M. A., & Goulden, M. (2004). Marriage and baby blues: Redefining gender equity in the academy. *Annals of the American Academy of Political and Social Science, 596,* 84–103.

Moen, P. (Ed.). (2003). *It's about time: Couples and careers.* Ithaca, NY: ILR Press.

Padavic, I., & Reskin, B. (2002). *Women and men at work,* 2d ed. Thousand Oaks, CA: Pine Forge Press.

Schwartz, F. (1989, January/February). Management women and the new facts of life. *Harvard Business Review,* pp. 65–76.

Williams, J. C. (2005, November). Are your parental-leave policies legal? *Chronicle of Higher Education, 51*(23), C1–C4.

❖ STUDENT RESPONSE

1. What is the difference between a *dual-career* and a *dual-earner* couple? Which of these terms describes Karen and Tim?

2. What are the advantages and disadvantages of a *dual-career* relationship? How are the advantages different from those of a couple that has a dual-earner relationship?

3. Should work life and family/personal life be integrated or separated? Explain. What are the advantages of integration and of separating work and family? How did Karen and Tim approach this issue?

4. What specific expectations, on the part of their employers, created the most problems for Tim and Karen? Do you think these are common in other professions?

5. Research the idea of "mommy tracks" (special career tracks for mothers) to become familiar with the concept. What is the purpose of mommy tracks? What does Karen mean when she says she "considered herself mommy-tracked"? Do you think mommy tracks are a good idea or not? Why?

6. What institutional policies might have helped Tim and Karen pursue both their careers and their desire for a family? Do you think their employers' attitudes, as expressed in their family policies or work demands, are typical of the contemporary workplace or not? (See the Appendices for some relevant policy information.)

7. In light of what the case reveals about Karen's and Tim's priorities, do you think they should have another child now or not? Why?

APPENDIX A: SUMMARY OF THE FAMILY AND MEDICAL LEAVE ACT (FMLA) OF 1993

The Family and Medical Leave Act (FMLA) of 1993 became effective August 5, 1993. The FMLA requires employers of 50 or more employees within a 75-mile area to provide up to 12 weeks of unpaid, job-protected leave to eligible employees for certain family and medical reasons. Employees are eligible if they have worked for a covered employer for at least one year and for 1,250 hours over the previous 12 months.

Reason for Taking Leave

An employer must grant unpaid leave to an eligible employee for any of the following reasons:

- for the care of the employee's child (birth or placement for adoption or foster care)
- for the care of the employee's spouse, son or daughter, or parent, who has a serious health condition
- for a serious health condition that makes the employee unable to perform her job

The employee may be required to provide advance leave notice and medical certification.

Job and Benefits Protection

Upon return from FMLA leave, most employees must be restored to their original or equivalent positions with equivalent pay, benefits, and other employment terms. The use of FMLA leave cannot result in the loss of any employment benefit that accrued prior to the start of an employee's leave.

SOURCE: United States Department of Labor, Wage and Hour Division. Retrieved August 25, 2006, at: www.dol.gov

APPENDIX B: FACTS ABOUT PREGNANCY DISCRIMINATION

The Pregnancy Discrimination Act is an amendment to Title VII of the Civil Rights Act of 1964. Discrimination on the basis of pregnancy, childbirth, or related medical conditions constitutes unlawful sex discrimination under Title VII. Women affected by pregnancy or related conditions must be treated in the same manner as other applicants or employees with similar abilities or limitations.

Hiring

An employer cannot refuse to hire a woman because of her pregnancy as long as she is able to perform the major functions of her job. An employer cannot refuse to hire her because of its prejudices against pregnant workers or the prejudices of coworkers, clients, or customers.

Pregnancy and Maternity Leave

An employer may not single out pregnancy-related conditions for special procedures to determine an employee's ability to work. An employer may, however, use any procedure that is used to screen other employees' ability to work. For example, if an employer requires its employees to submit a doctor's statement concerning their inability to work before granting leave or paying sick benefits, the employer may require employees with pregnancy-related conditions to submit such statements.

If an employee is temporarily unable to perform her job because of pregnancy, the employer must treat her the same as any other temporarily disabled employee; for example, by providing modified tasks, alternative assignments, disability leave, or leave without pay.

Pregnant employees must be permitted to work as long as they are able to perform their jobs. If an employee has been absent from work as a result of a pregnancy-related condition and recovers, her employer may not require her to remain on leave until the baby's birth. An employer may not have a rule that prohibits an employee from returning to work for a predetermined length of time after childbirth.

Employers must hold open a job for a pregnancy-related absence for the same length of time that jobs are held open for employees on sick or disability leave.

SOURCE: U.S. Equal Employment Opportunity Commission. Retrieved August 25, 2006, at: www.eeoc.gov/facts/fs-preg.html

APPENDIX C: RELEVANT POLICIES—
MIDWEST UNIVERSITY AND WORTH COLLEGE

Midwest University's Policy Regarding the Tenure Clock and Childbirth

Requests for extension of the probationary period (the period prior to granting of tenure) with respect to childbirth or adoption shall be submitted by the faculty member in writing to the Vice Chancellor for Academic Affairs (with informational copies to the faculty member's department chair and dean) within one year of the birth or adoption. Approval of the request for an extension of up to one year is presumed. The Vice Chancellor will notify the faculty member, department chair, and dean of the action taken.

More than one request may be granted because of responsibilities with respect to childbirth or adoption where more than one birth or adoption occurs during the probationary period. Where a leave of absence of six weeks or more has been granted for childbirth or adoption within one year of the birth or adoption, the total resulting extensions of the probationary period, for each birth or adoption, may not exceed one year.

Worth College's Assistant Professor Leave Policy

Worth has a program of leaves for assistant professors that provides a one-semester leave with support equivalent to full pay, for any eligible assistant professor who is deemed to have a worthy research or other creative project best supported by released time from teaching. Eligibility is restricted to assistant professors who have been reappointed to a four-year second term or whose initial appointments were for a term of more than three years. . . . Such leaves are most often granted in the person's fourth year at the College. . . . Assistant professors are expected to apply for grant funds available outside the College to help support the leave. . . . Should the assistant professor so wish, it may be possible to combine outside funding or a leave without pay with an assistant professor leave, in order to achieve a full-year leave of absence.

Note: This policy was *not* in effect during Karen's service at Midwest University

6

Kinder, Kirche, Küche

Working Mothers in Germany

CASE OVERVIEW

The case focuses on the business career of a contemporary female professional in Germany and highlights issues related to work and family. A variety of German public policies is relevant and affects the choices preferred and those avoided by German working women. The importance of wider cultural attitudes about family and the organizational culture in businesses also affect the woman's experiences and her worries. The setting is an informal discussion among a number of friends of various ages and family and work situations. The variations in culture between the former East Germany and former West Germany also enter the case.

❖ BODY OF CASE

Carlotta rushed toward the restaurant in downtown Berlin, where a group of her college friends was meeting for their annual help session and personal visit. In the past few years it had been harder and harder to convene the group, because of work demands for some (like her), geographic scattering, and family commitments among several. Nonetheless, they persisted, realizing the value of their mutual support. The group included Carlotta's four best friends; and in most ways their situations reflected those of many contemporary German women in their mid-thirties. Karin, the only native of former East Germany, who lived in that region still, was currently working full-time and was married without children. The others were Lily, an executive like Carlotta, but with no children; Friede, who worked part-time in an undemanding job in retail and had two children in elementary school; and Liz, also working part-time, with two teenaged children. Carlotta, an executive with a two-year-old daughter, looked forward fondly and eagerly to their conversation. She had been so stressed lately and needed some feedback.

Contemporary Realities

"Hi, everyone," Carlotta began as they settled in for the visit. "I am sure glad to see you; I've been so strung out lately, I can hardly think straight."

"What's up?" asked Lily, the other executive in the group.

"I just can't cope with the child-care situation much longer," Carlotta answered. "I leave her at the *kita* (daycare center) in the morning, but then they shut down promptly at 5:00 P.M., no exceptions, and we have to figure out how to cover at least two more hours, most days. Even if I worked normal hours—which I seldom can, as you're all aware—I would have to leave work an hour early to get to the *kita* on time. I was so lucky to get her into the *kita*, finally, but now I have to constantly try to find someone who can take her home and stay until one of us gets there. Even that new proposal from the government, calling for funding more daycare slots, is a minimal solution (Ziwica, 2004) and doesn't come close to covering a normal working day, which is usually eight or nine hours when you take into account travel times to and from work," she said.

"Yeah," said Lily. "It's no accident I haven't had a baby yet. Karl and I just can't see how it would work. Kids are real career killers in Germany, in spite of all the profamily, proworker rhetoric. Over 40% of female college grads like us, between 30 and 35, are now childless (Casagrande, 2004). And the child-care situation is just impossible. I think I'm probably going to be childless, just like most of my friends who want real careers."

Carlotta sighed. "I can see your point, now that I'm in the middle of all this and trying to cope," she responded. "And I even have a paid *kita*. Think of those families who can afford only the government-funded centers, which are currently open only four hours a day (Federal Statistical Office, 2003). They really have no choice but part-time work. But I can't imagine life without kids; I've always wanted and expected to be a mother. It makes me so angry that so many German women feel, now, that it's an either-or choice between meaningful work and a family. It just feels like the dark ages."

"It's worse for those in the former western sector of the country," argued Karin, their friend from the former East Germany. "We have the advantage in the East of all the child-care facilities that were developed during the communist era, when men and women were both very clearly expected to work, even with families. I read recently that in the eastern regions of Germany, 36% of children under the age of three have a daycare spot, while in the West, the percentage drops to a meager 2.7% (Drobnic, Blossfeld, & Rohwer, 1999). That's really a dramatic difference. Only about 57% of the couples in former West Germany have kids and, of those, 47% have only one. In the East, 50% of mothers work full-time but only 20% do in the West (*Marriage and Family*, n.d.). I feel as if Josef and I may decide after all to have a child, though I'm still pretty scared about what will happen to my career."

"Well that old East German attitude of supporting outside care of children certainly isn't the norm these days," chimed in Friede, who had two elementary-age children and worked part-time. "We all know that in the West family politics and policies took a different path. On the whole, politicians in the West always tended to view care outside the home by third parties with suspicion and instead opted for policies that encouraged women—for the first few years at least—to stay home. The mother-ideology of the Third Reich and the conservative women's politics after World War II have left deep marks," she explained. "The separation of the areas of public and private life was cemented with the exclusive responsibility of women for the private areas—caring for children and ensuring the welfare of the family."

"That traditional thinking is really still popular, perhaps even more so outside the cities," said Liz, the mother of two teenagers. "In rural areas they still use *rabenmutters* [uncaring mothers] as the word for women with children who work full-time. That awful term flourished in the 1930s through the heyday of the Nazi party. It seems to me that many of our government policies, though they sound liberal, work against women really having a career."

Carlotta agreed. "We're the world leader when it comes to not having kids," she said. "Lots of countries have low birthrates, but that so many people go without kids at all, and that so many of them are highly qualified workers—that's something you only see here in Germany."

"Well, that's probably related to both general attitudes and lack of services, plus maybe some bias in business, as well," argued Karin. "My friend Gilda works for a company that helped her find a kindergarten that stays open until 6:30 P.M., and helped her get her daughter Charlotte into it. They have a contract with an agency to help their employees with this stuff. And when the waiting list at the kindergarten was nine months, the company helped her move up on the list. They also give her the flexibility to arrange her day as it suits her. Some days, she leaves the office as early as 3:00 P.M. to pick up her daughter. But she also knows that if she has to work late, the kindergarten has business-friendly hours, meaning Charlotte is in good hands until 6:30 P.M. But only a very few companies do this sort of thing. You do hear, though, that more of them are getting worried about losing highly trained women after childbirth, so maybe there's some hope."

"Mine sure doesn't have that attitude," said Carlotta. "It's a U.S.-owned multinational, with major franchises in Europe. My superiors were great about maternity leave, but since I got back, they've just said forget it. Their concern for family situations is nil."

"The Ministry for Family Affairs offered a competition to name the country's top companies for parents. I hear more than 300 companies entered," said Lily (Corbett, 2005).

"Well, that new minister has been all over this issue," said Liz. "The other day she called Germany 'a third world country' when it comes to child care. That was when she introduced the new proposals" (Ziwica, 2004).

"Our maternity/paternity leave policies look great compared to those of many other countries," Carlotta said. "We can get up to three years off during the first 8 years of a child's life, and either parent can take portions of that amount of leave. And the first two years are at full salary and don't even include the 14 weeks of paid maternity leave. The U.S. policy doesn't require employers to pay for any family leave at all, and companies with few employees don't even have to provide family leave (U.S. Department of Labor, 2006). But my company, even though it's U.S.-controlled, had to comply with German law about this."

Friede jumped in here. "That's true, Carlotta, but that family leave is exactly what sets women up to not continue full speed ahead on a career. The traditional attitudes contribute also. I stayed home for three years with our first, then returned, but only part-time because of wanting to be a good mother. Then I did it again, after Robyn was born. They don't have to give you your same job back, of course, and they can even fire you four months after you return. In many jobs you will have already lost a lot of ground during the two to three years out— contacts, keeping up with your skills and your field, good assignments to develop your portfolio, and so on. Then if you go part-time on top of it, you've really settled for a much-reduced career. Of course, the company has also lost a lot of its initial investment of time and money in you. So even though half the college students are women, and 47% of the workforce is female, the reality is very much more complicated when you really analyze it."

"There's a tax angle, too," said Liz, referring to the persistence of the *kindergeld*—a federal income tax break that began in 1955 in West Germany. "That kindergeld really emphasizes the traditional gender roles. The break goes to married couples in which one of the couple— in practice it's usually the mother, of course—earns no salary. So before mine were in school, I stayed at home all the time, figuring the tax break at least partially offset the loss from not working part-time. I didn't go to even the part-time option until the youngest was in school, and so I was out of the work setting for eight years. Now that the kids are older, I'm finding it really hard to get back into full-time work, which I'd like at this point. And not as a store clerk, either, after all my education!"

Carlotta agreed. "Some of the younger women in my company really see that," she said. "They're very reluctant to step off the career ladder, for fear of having to start at the bottom again should they decide to return to work. And some others I know who've done it have found they're plagued by guilt, which goes back to the *rabenmutters* [uncaring mothers] stigma again."

"Which is why," Lily suggested, "we now have this political panic and debate about our social security system's solvency, just like the United States but for more complex reasons. In the United States the problem seems to be the size of the retiring generation and the smaller one just behind it. In Germany, it's the younger generation's decisions that may weaken things even more drastically further into the future. Our birthrate now's only 1.3 babies per woman of child-bearing age, far less than the 2.1 rate that experts say is needed to maintain a stable population. The big increase in living together before marriage has also pushed childbearing later into many women's lives (*Marriage and Family,* n.d.). We already don't finish a professional education until 30 or so, and that gives us a pretty small window of time to make the decision about kids. Some even joke we might become extinct at this rate, let alone being able to support future generations of retirees. At least in the United States people continue to have babies!" (Janes, 2006).

"True, Lily," said Karin. "The two problems seem to me to be clearly connected, which could be why the government is finally responding. Maybe that, combined with companies belatedly waking up about their own losses, may help. Companies really lose out if women decide to leave in order to raise a family—it's incredibly expensive and makes no sense. That's why some companies are starting to do something about it themselves" (Corbett, 2005).

"Well, I think German business has its own problems in all this," commented Friede. "Johann told me recently, when the first woman was appointed to the board of a blue-chip corporation—you remember, that woman in the pharmaceutical company—that only 7 of the 525 board positions in Germany's 100 leading companies are held by women. That's just ridiculous, and it can't *all* be due to child care!" (Leixnering, 2004).

"You're right, Friede," said Carlotta. "Companies also associate top jobs with male traits, like aggressiveness and so on. Women still play second fiddle in the business culture, and only about 4% of our senior managers are women (Leixnering, 2004). This also results, in part, from men being reluctant to hire capable young women, who might advance all the way to the top, because of their assumption that women won't stick with it. The business culture still is dominated by the traditional attitudes we talked about earlier."

"Well, I guess we should all have moved to Laer [small town in northwestern Germany]," said Karin. "Why?" asked Liz.

"They recognized that child care for our kids under three was almost nonexistent, and that nannies and au pairs are unpopular ideas here," Karin responded. "A bunch of parents, teachers, churches, and local authorities made concerted efforts to get a community plan. They convinced the mayor, who lobbied hard for money and community support. Now there is a town daycare center for toddlers and infants, and mothers take turns minding the children because they all want to work (Goldsmith, 2005). The children can stay all day, which as we know is rare. The town has grown tremendously, because people have moved there because of the center. The population is only 6,000 in the community and 1,000 of them are kids! And the mayor now sits on the new federal commission on children, in Berlin" (Ziwica, 2004).

"Well, that's great," Carlotta. "Unfortunately, moving there would take me further from this job, which in spite of everything, I just love."

Carlotta's Background and Career Development

While her friends were busy eating lunch and catching up, Carlotta mused about her career thus far. In many ways she had already been somewhat atypical of the women her age. She had gone to college, itself an opportunity very restricted in Germany, and proceeded to complete demanding professional training in economics and communication. As was true for many, she was 29 by the time she actually entered the workforce. For several years she had progressed through several private firms in Berlin, gaining greater responsibility with each move and building a strong background in general management to supplement her academic training. Her communication skills had proved very useful as she moved into more demanding management duties, taking responsibility for supervising others and relating to higher levels of management. She had actually assumed she would work awhile and then take a long absence, as many women do, including maternity leave when her children came along, and then perhaps even extending the absence or working part-time, like Friede, when her children entered elementary school.

A wrinkle had developed in this master plan, a plan so typical for German women; she had been unable to conceive a child. Her husband accepted the news with amazingly good grace, considering his expectations and those of both their families. He encouraged Carlotta to keep developing professionally and did not seem to mind being childless. About the time they both accepted the situation, a great opportunity presented itself for Carlotta, with the multinational Flow Corporation.

The company's European headquarters in Amsterdam had the idea of starting a branch of the business in Germany. Flow's philosophy is to open a new operation with the clients they already had, and their client base in Germany fit this model. The company provides technical service for computer and other technological firms, who contract out their customer service to Flow. In 1998 the company had done some business in Munich but was not successful, and so they closed the operation there. The managers were interested in Berlin because the governmental units in that city provided a lot of support services: Because of high unemployment, the government made grants to firms in support of salaries. It was established company policy to always hire local managers, and a headhunter found Carlotta working for a competitor and proposed her for the position. She realized it would be her biggest challenge to date, but it also offered a great jump in salary, prestige, and experience. She would be in complete charge of the Berlin technical support center, reporting to the European headquarters in Amsterdam, and through that office to the U.S. multinational headquarters in Massachusetts.

As luck would have it, Carlotta became pregnant less than 6 months after accepting this exciting and demanding new position. Nervous about the situation, she consulted her supervisor in Amsterdam. Somewhat to her surprise, he was quite accommodating. He knew the maternal/paternal leave policy in Germany required him to grant her absence, and she was able to take a year off when her daughter was born. The company brought in an experienced manager from elsewhere in Europe to cover her duties. Upon her return, it was agreed that she would take full responsibility again; the company was dedicated to operations managed by residents of the country in which the work was located, and management still believed Carlotta was their best prospect in Berlin.

She was by then responsible for all staffing, training, operations, and of course financial planning that kept the operation profitable. The recent downturn in Germany's economy—indeed, in the world economy—had forced her to make difficult decisions about laying off workers, operating the center at less than full capacity during the slow-down, and required increasingly frequent communication with superiors in both Amsterdam and the United States about the economic environment. All this of course substantially increased both her working hours and the stress of her job. (The databases used by the firm show the results of the operation every quarter-hour; this close accountability, with the instant oversight it provided, also was stressful, even though it also helped her manage the operation better.)

As her friends had pointed out earlier, it is unusual for a woman to hold such a high supervisory position in Germany. She knows she is the only woman in the Flow Corporation in Europe who is doing this level of work. It is sometimes uncomfortable, because she has 18 colleagues on the same level but she is the only female; she certainly would like female colleagues. It also means that there is really no one to understand, let alone support or help her solve, her child-care dilemmas. Even though *kita* slots are more available in Berlin than in other areas of the country, the hours pose great difficulties. Carlotta had to wait for nine months before her daughter could even be admitted. Right now, with her daughter two years old and another year away from kindergarten (which would involve another search for a scarce slot) Carlotta felt at her wit's end.

In her stress, she had consulted her superior to see if some different options might be worked out. She had asked about possibly working from home 1 day a week, or working fewer hours and hiring a professional assistant. Under the new child-care policies, employers were required to work out part-time arrangements unless it created undue stress on the company. Remembering the company's cooperation at the time of childbirth, Carlotta was hopeful. Her hopes were quickly dashed. Her superiors stressed the very competitive situation of the company and the need for absolute commitment from the top levels. "If you need part-time work or flexible locations and so on, you obviously will have to leave. Our environment's far too competitive to allow an executive that kind of leeway," said Carlotta's usually complimentary supervisor in Amsterdam.

She was still fascinated by her work, and in spite of the economic stress, had managed to make the hard decisions to keep the operation profitable even while coping with her new infant. She was quite confident that all these experiences were helping her really grow as a manager and that she could continue to advance in business. And things were beginning to improve, slowly, with the economy; but her child-care bind, with the added stress and guilt it sometimes produced, was proving intolerable.

What Are Carlotta's Choices?

"Well," said Friede, responding to what she had heard from Carlotta throughout the conversation, "I think you're just going to have to face reality like all the rest of us mothers. You need to step down to a less demanding, part-time position. Otherwise, you'll never know your daughter, and she will just bounce from school to babysitters and back again, with no real security. The cost is just too high; they only grow up once."

"I disagree," said Liz, chiming in. "That settling for part-time work is exactly what has ruined my chances; now that I want to work full-time, my skills are too rusty and the jobs I would like require more experience than I have. Don't fall into that trap! I think you should consider a nanny, and keep working full-time."

"Where would I get a nanny?" Carlotta asked. "So few come to Germany, because the market for them here is so weak, and the German girls all want to go abroad and have that experience. I wouldn't even know how to look for one."

"I would try the Ministry of Family Services, since they're currently so worked up about keeping us in the labor force," said Liz. "Or we can all ask our international friends if they have contacts in their home countries that might lead to a good nanny prospect."

"You also might look for a different company," said Karin, "such as the one I told you about earlier, that's making a real effort to help working moms line up services. I know this is like searching for a needle in a haystack in Germany, but your experience now is so valuable that other companies might be really interested in you."

"Yes, Carlotta," added Lily. "A job search might be warranted, since your company is being so unhelpful at the moment. You might find a firm that would be more flexible, in its hours and allowing some work from home, or even have a stimulating part-time position. Maybe you could even pressure your company, if you actually located another position, into making some adjustments for you."

"Those are good points," added Karin. "While we're thinking of possibilities, you might even consider starting a business of your own. There are quite a few women beginning to do that, now, and you have some really valuable experience at designing and running customer service operations. You might be able to sell yourself as a consultant on those matters, alone."

"I do have to be careful about the part-time idea, and being an entrepreneur carries all sorts of new risks with it," replied Carlotta. "Maybe I should just stick it out, since my prospects with this company seem really strong. Maybe things will get better when my daughter enters kindergarten. There's an awful lot to consider about all this. I guess you've all helped me clarify some options, but the picture still seems pretty bleak for female executives in Germany right now. I sure hope it's easier for our daughters!"

❖ RELATED READINGS

Casagrande, S. (2004, November 29). *Working women face upward battle.* Bonn: Deutsche Welle. Retrieved September 1, 2006, at: www.dw-world.de/dw/article/0,1564,1379189,00.html

Corbett, D. (2005, November 4). *Work-life balance gets boost in Germany.* Bonn: Deutsche Welle. Retrieved September 2, 2006, at: www.dw-world.de/dw/article/0,1564,1538716,00.html

Drobnic, S., Blossfeld, H.-P., & Rohwer, G. (1999, February 1). Dynamics of women's employment patterns over the family life course: A comparison of the United States and Germany. *Journal of Marriage & Family, 61*(1), 2422–2445.

Federal Statistical Office of Germany. (2003, June 12). *Microcensus 2002: 35% of all mothers, but not more than 3% of all fathers work part-time.* Press release.

Wiesbaden, Germany: Author. Retrieved September 2, 2006, at: www
.destatis.de/presse/englisch/pm2003/p2390024.htm

Goldsmith, R. (2005, June 15). *Laer leads German childcare revolution.* London:
BBC. Retrieved September 2, 2006, at: http://news.bbc.co.uk/2/hi/
programmes/crossing_continents/4095408.stm

Janes, J. (2006). *Forks in the reform roads in Germany and the U.S.* Washington,
DC: American Institute for Contemporary German Studies. Retrieved
September 2, 2006, at: www.aicgs.org/adaview.aspx?pageid=242

Leixnering, A. (2004, July 10). *For German women glass ceiling hangs low.* Bonn:
Deutsche Welle. Retrieved September 2, 2006, at: www.dw-world.de/dw/
article/0,2144,1263544,00.html

Marriage and family in Germany. (n.d.). Retrieved September 2, 2006, at:
www.germanculture.com.ua/library/facts/bl_marriage.htm

U.S. Department of Labor. (2006). *Leave benefits: Family and medical leave act.*
Retrieved September 2, 2006, at: www.dol.gov/dol/topic/benefits-
leave/fmla.htm

Vogelheim, E. (2005). The Alliance for Jobs in Germany: The promise and failure of gender mainstreaming. *Journal of Women, Politics & Policy, 27*(1/2),
163–173

Ziwica, K. (2004, July 21). *Germany struggles to close daycare gap.* Bonn: Deutsche
Welle. Retrieved September 2, 2006, at: www.dw-world.de/popups/
popup_printcontent/0,1272458,00.html

❖ STUDENT RESPONSE

1. What are some of the specific features of German society and
   German business that are contributing to Carlotta's dilemma?
   How do these complicate Carlotta's situation?

2. Several of Germany's policies are relevant to working mothers.
   Describe them and discuss how they seem to be affecting German
   women's careers and family choices.

3. Carlotta's friends have identified several options she might
   consider. Which of these do you prefer, and why? What are the
   advantages and disadvantages of each of the options?

4. The German government is concerned *both* about losing women
   (especially well-educated women) in the workforce and about the
   declining birthrate. What public policies do you think might help
   with these problems? How does one problem affect the other?

5. What does Carlotta's situation have in common with Karen's, in
   The Pregnant Professor case? How is Carlotta's situation different from Karen's?

7

Sexual Harassment in the Military

CASE OVERVIEW

This case presents descriptions of sexual harassment in the military from two perspectives: (1) problems at the U.S. military academies, which surfaced first at the Air Force Academy in the 2002–2004 period; and (2) incidents of harassment during the Iraq War in the same period. The case emphasizes the difficulties of changing an organizational culture that tolerates sexual harassment. It begins with a description of reported incidents of harassment and assault at the Air Force Academy, with subsequent studies and data indicating similar if less pervasive situations at the U.S. Army and U.S. Naval Academies. Next, the case reports numerous incidents in the Iraq and Afghanistan theaters of operation, and at a U.S. Air Force base at home, during the same time period. Historical references to similar incidents in the 1990s indicate that sexual harassment is a continuing problem in the U.S. military.

❖ BODY OF CASE

The group of Air Force cadets looked warily toward the school officials and representatives from the Department of Defense who had called them together. The officials were investigating recent reports of rape and sexual harassment at the Air Force Academy that had surfaced in the national media.

A sophomore cadet was charged with unlawful entry and indecent acts. His charges resulted from his entering of a woman's barracks after taps without her permission. Another cadet had recently been charged with entering a women's bathroom while cadets showered, and yet another had videotaped and photographed female cadets and stored images on his computer. As the scandal broke, dozens of women had come forward to report being raped at the academy in recent years.

"What we need," began one official, "are your own impressions of life for women at the academy. We are collecting data from a variety of sources, which will give us statistical information about how pervasive the problems are. But we need your insights into what may be contributing to the problems here."

"Until lately," Rachel contributed, "no one has paid any attention to these problems. We all have mandatory training about harassment when we arrive but no one takes it very seriously. This is a male place. The statue outside the academy sets the tone, with its inscription 'bring me men.'"

"I agree," Sarah added. "The emphasis here is on conforming and succeeding in a system of strict military discipline, and not asking for special treatment or consideration as a woman. The most important value is following the chain of command absolutely. When we are first-years, we really have trouble making any kind of independent judgment when upperclassmen tell us to do things. Many women believe they have to do what they're told—even if it involves breaking academy rules. You don't really question that. I know several cases where upperclassmen have pressured first years into breaking the rules (drinking, for example), and then threatened to report them if sexual favors were not granted."

"Why don't women report these incidents?" asked an academy representative. "I really can't agree that administration officials condone this behavior."

"There are lots of reasons," Lindsay stated. "The younger women, not in the chain of command, are afraid of reprisals from other upperclassmen, if incidents are reported. Upperclassmen sometimes abuse their power and use their influence to shun women who complain.

Lots of us also think the commanders really won't believe us, that somehow they will blame us for the incident; they never believe cadets over upperclassmen. If we have broken rules, we are also afraid of the punishment for doing that; this adds to the upperclassmen's influence over us in a harassment incident. We are so afraid of getting into trouble," she added, "that we don't exercise common sense."

Rachel agreed. "I think many women also fear nothing will be done, and they will have suffered embarrassment, and ostracism by their peers, probably punished by the commanders, with no positive result. These incidents always leak out, and then the victim herself is the one who suffers. The general tone of the place tends to be more supportive of men and see women who have problems as weak in some way, or complainers. I also know of incidents where the harassers basically escaped judgment, or received a 'slap on the wrist.'"

"That's why most of the harassment has not been reported. There really is no confidence in the system, or trust that those in charge want the harassment stopped or see it as a serious problem," Sarah added.

"Do you think most of the harassment is simply a result of a 'few bad apples' who abuse their power in the chain of command? Is this just like other college situations, where young women are vulnerable to older students' social pressure? Or do you see it differently?" asked the Department of Defense official.

"Well, these problems are certainly not limited to the academy," said Lindsay. "Remember the Air Force base where two dozen rapes were reported over a 12-month period? When that base was investigated, junior personnel said they were afraid of reprisals and afraid of being disciplined for misconduct such as underage drinking. They also worried about embarrassment, loss of confidentiality, and peer pressure. So they didn't report the rapes. Later, surveys showed that many women did not regard the base as a safe place to be."

"And what about all the incidents coming out of the Central Command area surrounding Iraq?" asked Rachel. "An Army officer recently testified before Congress that she had faced two sexual assaults and a spoken sexual intimidation in her 3 years on active duty in that theater of operations. Her most recent assault had taken place in Kuwait, less than a month after she was deployed to Iraq. She said the abuse and the 'repeatedly dismissive response to her complaints' had placed her future as an officer on hold. Several other military women at those congressional hearings described rapes occurring during a missile attack alert and one by an officer of another country's forces. Women were reluctant to report abuse for fear of being isolated within their units and having their chances for advancement hindered. There were more than 100 reports of sexual misconduct by members of the United States military in Iraq, Kuwait, Afghanistan, and Bahrain."

"So clearly these issues are not confined to the Air Force Academy or the Air Force itself," concluded the Department of Defense official. "The problems surfaced in the 1990s and were addressed with new training requirements, but now here they are again, at all the academies and in the regular forces as well. We have to get a handle on this once again, and do better."

❖ NEW QUESTIONS ON AN OLD PROBLEM

The military has in recent decades seen repeated episodes of mass accusations of sexual harassment and assault, punctuated by programs struggling to respond effectively and warnings of more problems to come. Early in 1991, the Navy's Tailhook scandal saw more than 80 women report assaults by drunken male aviators at a convention in a Las Vegas hotel. Two years later, a number of complaints caused the Air Force Academy to institute changes, including an increase in sensitivity training and the establishment of a hot line for reporting sexual assaults. (In reflecting on the incidents uncovered in 2003, the former academy superintendent who implemented changes in the 1990s said, "It's likely the processes we set up at that time may be outdated for a variety of reasons.")

In 1995, shortly before another rash of incidents was exposed at the Army's Aberdeen Proving Ground in Maryland, the government's General Accounting Office warned in a report that women at the military academies were facing widespread hostility, and that 70 to 80% said they had experienced recurrent sexual harassment. A few years later, in 1999, a group commissioned by Congress issued a report describing how the military should improve its processing of sexual crime accusations, including treating every one as a criminal matter, training investigators more thoroughly, and blocking the involvement of high-ranking officers in the implicated institutions.

The incidents in the 2002–2004 period reveal a continuing or resurgent problem, however. After the Air Force Academy problems were uncovered in 2003, new training was instituted at that academy, and eight high-ranking administrators who served during the years reviewed were demoted and/or removed from their positions. A study by the inspector general of the Department of Defense had revealed that nearly 12% of the women who graduated from the Air Force Academy in 2003 were the victims of rape or attempted rape while at the academy, and the vast majority never reported the incidents to the authorities.

A survey of 579 women at the academy found that nearly 70% of them said they had been the victims of sexual harassment, of which 22% said they experienced pressure for sexual favors. More than half the women surveyed said they believed the previous leadership of the academy failed to properly handle the sexual assault problem (CNN, August 29, 2003).

The inspector general's report said that sexual assaults against women were reported almost 150 times over 10 years but that little action was taken until the accusations became public in 2003. "We conclude that the overall root cause of sexual assault problems at the Air Force Academy was the failure of successive chains of command to acknowledge the severity of the problem," wrote the inspector general in a letter accompanying the report. "Consequently, they failed to initiate and monitor adequate corrective measure to change the culture until recently," he added (*New York Times*, December 8, 2004). A civilian commission appointed to study the problem echoed these findings and said that sexual assault had been a problem at the academy throughout the last decade—and possibly since women were first admitted, in 1976 (*New York Times*, December 8, 2004).

Congress also commissioned research at both the U.S. Army Academy at West Point and the U.S. Naval Academy at Annapolis and required annual surveys to measure sexual harassment and assault at all three of the academies. Incidents continued to occur at all the academies. In 2005 results of surveys at the three academies revealed that more than 50% of female respondents and 11% of male respondents indicated experiencing some type of sexual harassment after entering the schools: 176 incidents in which "private parts" were "touched, stroked, or fondled" without consent and 127 incidents in which someone physically attempted to have sexual intercourse but was not successful had occurred during the previous school year (Associated Press, March 18, 2005). At West Point 6% of the female cadets experienced sexual assault, 41% reported them, and 39% of those 41% said they experienced repercussions; 62% of the females experienced sexual harassment, and 61% of females and 58% of males said sexual assault and harassment training was slightly or not at all effective. In the same year, 5% of female midshipmen at Annapolis experienced sexual assault, 40% reported it, and 59% of the females experienced sexual harassment. At the Air Force Academy, 4% of the females experienced sexual assault in the 2004 academic year, 44% of them reported it, and 49% of the 4% experienced sexual harassment. On the other hand, 81% of the females and 87% of the males said sexual assault was less of a problem than when they enrolled (Associated Press, December 23, 2005). Women at all the academies reported that fellow cadets and midshipmen were the offenders, that assaults occurred most often in dormitories and barracks, and that they did not report assaults because they feared public disclosure, ostracism, harassment, ridicule, and not being believed.

Other studies revealed the extent of the problems in the military as a whole. Studies of the Air Force base mentioned earlier by the cadet at the academy revealed 114 incidents of sexual assault at that one base over a 10-year period, including 5 cases of gang rapes, with substantial delays in processing evidence and pursuing charges against reported offenders (*Denver Post,* February 29 and March 12, 2004). The Department of Defense acknowledged data from the Central Command surrounding Iraq indicating more than 100 reported cases of sexual misconduct in that theater of operations in an 18-month period (Stout, 2005). Also according to the Department of Defense, one sixth of 1% of deployed female service members are victims of an attempted or actual rape. Research from the Department of Veteran Affairs in 2003 indicated that one third of former military women treated at Veterans Affairs medical centers reportedly suffered rape or attempted rape during their military service. The Veterans Administration concluded that one third of females deployed during Desert Storm and Desert Shield were challenged by physical sexual harassment, and a comparative analysis indicates that rate was 10 times as great as the civilian rate during the same time period.

These and other data compiled in response to events early in the new century prompted a number of efforts by the military establishment to again try to address the sexual harassment and assault problems, both at the service academies and throughout the military services.

❖   THE LATEST PROPOSALS: WILL THEY WORK?

A special defense task force on sexual harassment and violence at the military service academies, commissioned by Congress, made its recommendations in June of 2005. These are summarized in its report and emphasize the following points. "Some in the academy communities do not value women as highly as men." One recommendation is to increase the number and visibility of female officers and noncommissioned officers in key positions to serve as role models for both male and female cadets and midshipmen and to increase the percentage of women cadets and midshipmen at the academies. Regular surveys to document attitudes and behaviors related to women are also urged by the task force. Since confidentiality for victims is a problem, Congress is encouraged to create a statutory privilege protecting the communications made by victims of sexual assault to health-care providers and victim advocates. The academies are also urged to further maximize the use of existing and potential avenues for victims' support and reporting. Training on sexual harassment and assault should be integrated into general coursework that is graded, to increase the seriousness of such training and spread it more widely throughout the curriculum. Education should be mandatory, conducted at various levels over the course of cadets' and midshipmen's four-year career at the academies, and conducted by qualified faculty members. To increase the accountability of offenders, Congress should revise the current sexual misconduct laws to more clearly and comprehensively address the full range of sexual misconduct. The task force also recommends that the Uniform Code of Military Justice be amended to permit commanders to close proceedings on sexual assault and misconduct, to protect the privacy of victims and alleged offenders. All academies should develop an institutional sexual harassment and assault prevention plan that is evaluated and updated annually. Finally, a series of proposals recommend collaborative relationships with civilian authorities for support of sexual assault victims; these relationships should be formally endorsed by the academies and validated through official documentation. The task force argued against a "fix and forget" approach, urging support for these efforts from the military services, the civilian leadership of the Department of Defense, and Congress to ensure success.

In this regard, the Department of Defense also acted in 2005 to endorse new strategies across the military services, including the academies. Acknowledging serious flaws in how it has dealt with sexual assaults within the military, the Pentagon announced steps directed at preventing the crimes, investigating them more thoroughly when they occur, and treating victims with more consideration. "The department understands that our traditional system within each service does not afford sexual-assault victims the care and support they need across the board, and we are putting new systems in place to address this shortcoming, " David S. C. Chu, Undersecretary of Defense for personnel and readiness, said at a Pentagon briefing in 2005 (Stout, 2005).

A major part of the new policy is the appointment of a sexual assault response coordinator at every U.S. military installation in the world. This coordinator is charged with following a case from accusation through resolution, with particular attention to helping the victim.

A typical coordinator might be a high-ranking officer, someone who can "deal effectively with a base commander," according to department spokespersons. Military personnel will be educated on the new procedures up and down the chain of command, with commanders having ultimate responsibility. The coordinator will know the identity of a person making a complaint and the accused, but a commander will not, at least in the early stages, as the new policy is envisioned. Mr. Chu acknowledged how difficult it could be to make changes within the military culture, which until relatively recently was overwhelmingly male.

Back at the Air Force Academy, Department of Defense representatives posed a question to the assembled cadets. "What do you think of all these new proposals, for the academies and for the military as a whole? Are we on the right track here? Will these ideas work?"

❖ RELATED READINGS

Burlington Industries, Inc. v. Ellerth, 524 U.S. 742 (1998). Retrieved August 25, 2006, at: www.oyez.org/oyez/resource/case/1109

Crist, G. (2003, May 9). Upperclassmen's power theme in AFA sex probe. Rocky Mountain News, p. 30A.

de Vise, D. (2005, March 19). Defense Dept. surveys academy sexual assaults. Washington Post, p. A1.

Graham, B. (1996, June 15). At least half of military women face harassment, despite falloff. Washington Post, p. A1.

Graham, B. (2004, February 26). Military faulted on assault cases. Washington Post, p. A19.

Meritor Savings Bank, PSB v. Vinson, 477 U.S. 57 (1986). Retrieved August 25, 2006, at: www.oyez.org/oyez/resource/case/240

Military academies faulted in harassment. (2005, August 26). Washington Post, p. A11.

Moffeit, M. (2003, March 26). 79 percent of female veterans report being sexually harassed. Denver Post, p. A8.

Pennsylvania State Police v. Suders, 542 U.S. 129 (2004). Available: http://www.oyez.org/oyez/resource/case/1714

Rank's role in harassment cases. (2000, May 18). Washington Post, p. A26.

Report of the Defense Task Force on Sexual Harassment and Violence at the Military Service Academies. (2005). Retrieved September 2, 2006, at: www.dtic.mil/dtfs/doc_recd/High_GPO_RRC_tx.pdf

Senate Committee on Armed Services. (2004). Allegations of sexual assault at the U.S. Air Force Academy. S. Hrg. 108-652. CIS-NO: 2004-S201–13. Washington, DC: U.S. Government Printing Office.

Senate Committee on Armed Services. (2005). Policies and programs for preventing and responding to incidents of sexual assaults in the armed services. S. Hrg. 108-799. CIS-NO: 2005-S201–11. Washington, DC: U.S. Government Printing Office.

Stout, D. (2005, January 5). Pentagon toughens policy on sexual assault. *New York Times*, p. A21.

U.S. Merit System Protection Board. (1995, October). *Sexual harassment in the federal workplace: Trends, progress, continuing challenges.* Washington, DC: U.S. Government Printing Office.

❖ STUDENT RESPONSE

1. Review the *Report of the Defense Task Force on Sexual Harassment and Violence at the Military Service Academies*. Do you think that the proposals are directed at the problems raised in the case? Do you think they are realistic?

2. The military repeatedly developed and required training programs during the 1990s to address sexual harassment issues, yet the problems resurfaced in the next decade. How are the proposals announced in 2005 different? Do you think the new proposals have a better chance of succeeding? Why or why not?

3. What is difficult about eliminating sexual harassment in the military? Why do the problems persist?

4. Why are women so hesitant to report harassment or assault within the military? What do you think is needed to change this pattern of nonreporting?

5. Review definitions and interpretations of sexual harassment in the Appendix and the court cases listed in Related Readings. Sexual harassment has been defined by the U.S. Supreme Court as including a hostile work environment as well as overt sexual behaviors and quid pro quo harassment. How might a hostile environment be related to the incidents described in the military case?

APPENDIX: DEFINITIONS OF SEXUAL HARASSMENT

Sexual harassment is a form of sex discrimination that violates Title VII of the Civil Rights Act of 1964 (and the 1991 amendments to that act).

"*Unwelcome* sexual advances, requests for sexual favors, and other verbal or physical conduct of a *sexual nature* constitutes sexual harassment when submission to or rejection of this conduct *explicitly or implicitly affects an individual's employment,* unreasonably interferes with an individual's work performance or creates an intimidating, *hostile or offensive work environment*" (U.S. Equal Employment Opportunity Commission, 1997. Retrieved September 2, 2006, at: www.eeoc.gov/types/sexual_harassment.html).

The key concepts in harassment thus are the sexual nature of the behavior; its unwelcome nature; intent versus impact of the behavior (impact is what matters); inappropriate use of power; and the "reasonable person standard"—meaning the behavior is offensive to a reasonable person—the standard that is used by the courts in hostile environment cases.

There are two broad categories of sexual harassment: *quid pro quo ("this for that") harassment,* and *hostile environment* harassment. *Quid pro quo* harassment often involves

- Employment decisions or expectations are implicitly or explicitly based on the employee giving or denying sexual favors.
- The person initiating the behavior is positioned with the authority to make job-related threats or promises.
- The employment decisions affected include hiring decisions, salary increases, shift schedules, work assignments, performance expectations, and the like.

Examples: demanding sexual favors in return for the promise of a raise; firing someone because they ended a relationship with the supervisor; changing job performance ratings for refusing to date the manager.

Hostile environment sexual harassment incorporates the following:

- The behavior focuses on the sexuality of another person or occurs because of the person's gender.
- The behavior is severe or pervasive enough that it interferes with job performance or creates an atmosphere that is considered abusive.
- A "reasonable person" would also have been offended.
- Anyone in the workplace might participate in the behavior, whether men or women, agents of the employer, coworkers, or nonemployees frequently at the work site.

Examples: sexual jokes; sexual comments; sexual pictures or cartoons; leering, staring; lewd gestures; excessive romantic attention; repeated requests for dates; touching, including brushing, hugging, patting, pinching, rubbing; groping, grabbing, fondling; sexual assault, rape. All the above are harassment if they are serious, pervasive, and unwelcome.

Conclusion

Five Issues, or Maybe Just One?

B etty Friedan, the founder of the National Organization for Women, who died in 2006, is widely credited with igniting the modern women's movement with the publication in 1963 of *The Feminine Mystique*. In discussing the "problem that has no name," this early work defined the challenges of women at mid-twentieth century, as they struggled for equality in several spheres and for the development of fulfilling lives of their own. Ms. Friedan (1997) more recently argued that America's *current* workplace problems seriously threaten the health of families and require a new paradigm of work and family life. Economic justice, rather than "narrow identity politics," was the basis for continuing women's and men's progress toward equality in the 1990s, she argued, and for the just treatment of children in society, as well. The notions of work equity and gender reflected in these two works—more than 30 years apart—provide an illuminating backdrop to the gender and workplace issues raised here. In particular, the complex interconnections between issues of workplace equity and the nature of family life are becoming clear (Jacobs & Madden, 2004).

The cases in this volume have each illustrated one area of gender concern in the contemporary workplace. In reality, however, the five sorts of issues covered are very intertwined and affect each other in a great many most significant ways. A brief review of the components of each situation in the cases will make this point clear.

In Half a Pie, or None? Kirsten Andersen sought to advance her already successful professional life to the level of top management in a major corporation. She intended to do so by acquiring a specific set of new skills and experience, which she believed would then lead logically to top management positions. Her immediate problem, as described in the case, was a pervasive gender stereotyping of the specific position she sought. Her situation, however, reflects several other gender-related workplace issues. For example, her inability to move into an evaluator's position effectively blocked her advancement into the management level she sought; in this way she was encountering a glass ceiling within the organization. In addition, it appeared that she carried on her career-planning efforts entirely on her own; at no point did she seem to have effective mentoring. Her strongest organizational supporter, Mr. Green, seemed fairly ineffective when her crises developed, though she did continue to seek his advice. Finally, while there was certainly no overt sexual harassment in this case, it is possible that the strict stereotyping of work in the organization was related to other behaviors that might constitute a hostile environment.

In One Step Forward, Two Steps Back? we can see sexual stereotyping in another culture, Chinese, since Jin Xiaoqin's original dreams of becoming a foreign service officer were denied to all women. In addition, though, issues related to family responsibilities, especially the provision of scarce benefits such as housing, also affected her career choices. Maintaining these secure benefits for herself continued to affect her choices, even when her family assumed a less prominent role in her life. Glass ceiling dynamics may also have been present, as her advancement in her academic post seemed to have come to a stop for lack of the foreign service experience that had been denied her.

In the attorney's case, Meghan Evans, in her attempts to achieve a legal partnership, most obviously wrestled with the possible existence of a glass ceiling in her firm. But issues of career development and mentoring were also very relevant to Meghan's experience. The support of partners is clearly critical to achieving a legal partnership, and it is unclear whether Meghan had staunch supporters. No partners appeared in the case as active advisers to Meghan, possibly indicating a dearth of mentoring for her. The assignment of prominent legal cases is also a career development issue raised in her situation.

Meghan is charged with the financial and emotional responsibility of her two children. While the case does not suggest that this family role complicated her legal work, it is certainly possible that it did. Problems in the firm related to taking childbirth leave, and on-call work demands, even for part-time and for male as well as female attorneys, suggest a culture not attuned to family concerns. The six-year time frame for achieving partnership might have conflicted with the responsibilities of parenting in a number of ways at certain ages of Meghan's children during that period, and their situations and needs. Potential sexual harassment is also included in Meghan's situation, in the references to offensive behavior of several attorneys in the firm. The attempt to change Meghan's area of legal expertise to family law may also indicate a problem of gender stereotyping within her firm. Thus, while Meghan's case is an interesting example of possible glass ceiling issues and their complexity, each of the other gender-related issues may also be present in her workplace environment and may affect her progress toward the partnership she seeks.

The physicians in Medical Mentoring were also subject to a complex interplay of gender issues. The focus of their discussion was upon the need for early sponsorship into desirable specialties and positions and the difficulties they faced in acquiring this essential mentoring and assistance from senior physicians. They were also encountering issues related to compensation and advancement, however, as they debated at some length the reasons for their earnings being lower than those of male physicians and the difficulties of advancing into the top positions of medical school faculty and administration. Clearly, balancing family responsibilities with the demands of the practice of medicine was also difficult for many of these women. Sexual harassment, though not mentioned in this case, is present in the experiences of female medical students (Komaromy, Bindman, Haber, & Sande, 1993). Again, the gender issues affecting these women doctors are complex and interconnected.

Tim and Karen, the academic couple in The Pregnant Professor, also encountered a mix of gender issues in their early work and family experiences. The focus of their case was clearly upon the competing pressures they experienced from combining their chosen academic and policy careers with establishing a family. Karen also needed help, however, in defining (and redefining) her long-term career goals, and the availability of a mentor for even a brief period appeared important in helping her to revise her career goals. Her husband also made several career-planning readjustments in the period examined in the case, though it is unclear whether he received mentoring as an aid in that process. (It is interesting that their *initial* mentor in graduate school, an academic, presented their prospects in a most discouraging light, essentially telling them both that their careers and marriage were incompatible.) Research suggests that professors who are parents work fewer hours than nonparents and also express less job dissatisfaction. The authors of one study suggest that "parents [especially mothers] are less likely to put in these very long [60 hours per week] hours . . . [and] the tension between work and family does not end with young children or achieving tenure" (Jacobs, Madden, & Winslow, 2004, p. 127). There is also evidence, however, that many *female* faculty (about 40%

at this writing) are childless, presumably in part because of the work expectations. Advancement issues also applied to Karen's situation as she struggled with the high expectations for faculty seeking tenure at Midwest University and the informal culture of her department toward "having a life" and commitment to work.

In Germany, Carlotta's situation has both similarities to and differences from those faced by professionals in the United States who are parents. The public policies of the German government make a big difference in how mothers approach their professional choices, and German cultural attitudes toward women's roles also seem to be somewhat more traditional than is currently the case in the United States. It is clear, though, that here again there is more than one gender issue combining to affect women's careers. The German women in the case cite advancement difficulties as well as parenting issues. They also suggest some organizational barriers to advancement and possible stereotyping of the assignments women are given, particularly after they become mothers.

Finally, Sexual Harassment in the Military, while graphically documenting the extent and nature of sexual harassment, also raises issues of career development and advancement as well as the need for a sort of mentoring. It is clear that the primary victims of the harassment in the case need someone in whom to confide (other than chain-of-command personnel), which is an indication of the need of a younger woman for the support and advice of a more senior one. The women in the case—whether at the academies or on active military duty—are also afraid of being excluded from advancement if they actively object to the harassment they experience. While family concerns are not raised in the case, it is certainly arguable that the structure of military careers and assignments is still quite difficult to combine with the role of wife and mother, especially if the individuals involved retain a more traditional definition of those roles.

It is entirely possible, then, that a woman encountering sexual harassment in the military might also be affected by issues of career development and mentoring, promotion and compensation issues, balancing family roles with a military career, and possible gender stereotyping of potential assignments. Her choices about one of these issues—here, sexual harassment—could both affect and be affected by the others.

Friedan's (1963) early phrase, "the problem that has no name," became a shorthand expression of the issues of gender inequality in the 1960s and 1970s. While subsequent analysis and discussion of gender issues has become more precise and detailed, it is possible that lumping the issues together has some real validity. For, as seen in these few cases, the gender issues in the contemporary workplace are inextricably intertwined. Further, as Friedan (1997) would suggest, these issues affect the work and personal lives of men and, increasingly, their children as well (Jacobs & Madden, 2004). So perhaps, after all, it is *one* problem—albeit one with many facets—as Friedan argued.

❖ ORGANIZATIONAL CULTURE

The cases here point out another significant feature of gender issues in the workplace. The specific nature of a particular issue, the form it takes, and the options and means available for addressing it are different in different organizations and informal work cultures. This is even more apparent in many international settings, where cultures differ dramatically and constrain available and effective options in unique ways. Of special value in understanding how organizational culture develops, can be recognized, and changes is Edgar Schein's important work, *Organizational Culture and Leadership* (2004). His premises provide a basis for examining the importance of organizational culture in the gender-related workplace issues addressed here.

Leaders in organizations, according to Schein, initially create the culture of those organizations. Subsequently, however, the culture is owned by the organization, and the culture helps create new leaders. When organizations experience major difficulties or adaptive problems, the leaders must step *outside* the prevailing culture to start the process of change. This process, if successful, redefines the part of the culture that is nonfunctional or problematic.

Organizational culture is defined by Schein as containing the following elements: patterns of interaction, basic norms of behavior, the espoused values of the group, its formal philosophy, the rules of the game or ropes in the organization, the atmosphere or climate of work and the feelings related to that, shared meanings, and integrating symbols of the organization (Schein, 2004, pp. 12–13). A culture exists in an organization when a group has enough shared history to form a set of shared assumptions (p. 30). Schein also asserts that if leaders are not "conscious of the cultures in which they are embedded, those cultures will manage them" (p. 23).

Much of what is readily observed in organizations, according to this analysis, is an organization's artifacts: that is, "the visible organizational structures and processes," which include "its physical environment, language, technology and products, its style and the organizational processes into which such behavior is made routine" (Schein, 2004, p. 26). This part of an organization is easy to observe but difficult to interpret. In particular, Schein cautions against attempting to infer the meaning of artifacts, since one's own values inevitably are fed into such interpretations. Rather, Schein suggests that the effective analysis must get beyond the artifacts to two additional levels of culture.

"Espoused values," which are present through the expression of the values of leaders, and initially followed by others as a way to proceed, constitute the first of these additional levels of culture. If these espoused values become effective for the group, in enhancing their work and creating progress toward goals, then the values are transformed in "shared basic assumptions" (Schein, 2004, p. 30). When a solution to a problem works repeatedly, it comes to be taken for granted and is very hard to confront or change (p. 31).

In time, people in the organization accept these values so thoroughly that they are no longer confronted, debated, or questioned. Like Thomas Kuhn's (1970) notion of "paradigm," basic assumptions cause individuals to perceive reality so that it is congruent with the assumptions, even if doing so requires self-delusion. Basic assumptions thus become very difficult to change. It is only through leaders who can, at least temporarily, step outside the prevailing culture that new, innovative approaches can be suggested and tried. This brings us back, of course, to the initial step in organizational culture formation, that of leadership proposals.

Because individuals and groups place a high value on stability, changing an organization's basic assumptions—which is the key to changing its culture—is a very long and difficult process. As Schein (2004) points out, "The most central issue . . . is how to get at the deeper levels of a culture, how to assess the functionality of the assumptions made at each level, and how to deal with the anxiety that is unleashed when those levels are challenged" (p. 37). Many other scholars as well have documented the importance of these basic concepts to the process of organizational change. Goldin (1990) in her analysis of women's economic progress, for example, writes that "change is often stymied by institutions, norms, stereotypes, expectations, and other factors that serve to impose the past on the present" (p. 9). Since the gender issues in the workplace examined here are clearly a result of the basic cultures of a variety of work organizations and professions, they highlight the importance of using these ideas to understand the problems at hand, their underlying causes, and potential means for accomplishing change.

Although it is not possible to fully analyze the basic assumptions of each of the organizations included in the cases here, a brief reexamination of the organizations reinforces the importance of organizational culture to the gender issues raised. In Half a Pie there was clearly a basic assumption, at least on the part of a few top managers, that women are inappropriate candidates for the very demanding work of evaluators. The precise reasons for this stereotype were never clearly acknowledged by those who espoused it; nonetheless, since no women held this position, and women continued to be denied access to it, it seems clear that *some* underlying assumption must have been reinforcing the organizational artifact of denying women these positions. Mr. Green's reluctance, despite his personal support of Ms. Andersen, to confront his organization is further evidence that an important underlying value was influencing behavior on this matter.

Students may have identified some possible means of attempting to affect the procedures and other artifacts of the culture that were blocking Ms. Andersen and other women from this work. Schein's (2004) contribution, however, would argue that, in addition to attacking the artifacts both within and outside the organization—through legal action, for instance—leaders committed to solving this problem in a more permanent way would have to challenge the prevailing assumption that is facilitating the behavior. In the case, no leader really appeared willing to take on this challenge, although the new CEO, near the end of the case, indicated that he might do so in the future.

Thus, Mr. Green and Ms. Andersen, throughout the case, had a variety of choices about her situation; few of them would permanently affect the organization, however, unless basic assumptions in the culture were challenged at the same time. Nevertheless, individual actions remain important, since the cumulative impact of many *individual* challenges to the culture may, in time, provide ammunition for subsequent leaders to prove to others that the current assumptions are unworkable.

In the Chinese case, less was known about the attitudes and behaviors of other actors in blocking women's access to foreign service careers. Because of the political climate of the time, however, and because the government imposed the rule, the commitment of very highly placed individuals, indeed, would have been necessary to change the prevailing attitudes and practices of the Chinese Foreign Service. It is not an accident, then, that Jin Xiaoqin did not challenge her situations in the way that Kirsten Andersen attempted to challenge hers. Using Schein's (2004) analysis, there was no commitment among the organizational leaders to try to change the existing organizational culture. This remained true throughout the several decades of experience spanned in Jin's career.

Similarly, Meghan Evans's experience in seeking promotion to partner was fundamentally affected by the organizational culture in her law firm. The espoused values related to the evaluation of the work of associates were reflected in the evaluation process used by the firm and the comments of the various partners on Ms. Evans's work. Further, the firm espoused a thorough evaluation, standardized in form, and at least somewhat quantitative in nature, as its reflection of the value of fairness. The case also makes clear that the firm denied gender bias in both its operating procedures and its underlying assumptions.

Not clear, however, is the place of the espoused value of legal analytical ability within the firm's value structure. Some of the partners believed that this ability was a *sine qua non* for partners, an absolute essential, while other data in the case, particularly some of the judgments about male associates, indicated that weakness in one legal area might perhaps be compensated for by strength in another. Ms. Evans's difficulty in establishing gender bias in her evaluation process, after the initial court ruling, reflected the complexity of analyzing the firm's underlying basic assumptions; it was unclear whether systematic gender bias was, as Ms. Evans claimed, a feature of the firm's organizational culture.

In this case, the evaluation process used to select partners was a crucial artifact of the firm's culture, but, as Schein's (2004) model would suggest, the most essential part of the analysis involves determining the basic assumptions of the firm, which is not possible to do simply using the artifacts. The Epilogue's (see Instructor's Manual) allusion to the number of partners exiting the firm after the time frame of this case might suggest dissatisfaction with the firm's prevailing organizational culture, although the specific reasons for the unusual number of disaffections are not provided. The suggested analysis (in the Student Response) of the actions that partners and future associates might take, in an attempt to improve the organizational climate for women in the firm, once again suggests the importance of individual leaders in promoting change in the culture.

Medical Mentoring describes situations of young women physicians that are a direct reflection of the current culture of the medical profession. The long hours worked in medical practices and the necessity of sponsorship by more senior physicians in the key specialties, in particular, reflect underlying assumptions about what makes a good medical practitioner. Another issue raised in the case, the slow rate of advancement of women on medical school faculties, is an important artifact of those institutions and how they determine advancement. It may or may not reflect underlying bias against women in leadership roles in medical schools.

Of particular importance to the sponsorship issue raised in the case is the socialization process through which norms of a specialty are learned. The senior practitioners in the medical specialties serve as gatekeepers, effectively determining who gains admission to that specialty. Once accepted by a senior practitioner, then, the young physician learns much about that field of practice, makes important contacts, and so on, as a result of his or her mentoring. The individual values of these gatekeepers, then, effectively determine who enters the field and what they are taught about its practices. The women in the case, therefore, correctly determined that obtaining such sponsorship was vital to their success. The ultimate power to change the situation, however, clearly rests in the hands of the senior physicians. It is these individuals who would need to confront the prevailing norm of male dominance of the desired specialties, if the overall pattern is to be changed. Schein's (2004) emphasis upon the critical role of leaders in changing an organizational culture is thus very relevant to this case.

The discussion of balancing family and professional demands in Medical Mentoring suggested that at least some of the satisfied women physicians in the case were successful because they created their own organizations (medical practices) in which they could then define their schedules, volume of work, and so on, by themselves or with a similarly minded partner. This is another option for circumventing a prevailing organizational culture—by creating a new organization. The founders, then, as Schein's (2004) work suggests, have the freedom to impose their own values on the new culture, at least at the outset. When these values prove effective for the organization—as in the case of one of the medical practices described in Medical Mentoring—they then become embedded in the organization as its basic assumptions. Thus, Dr. Marcia Birthright and her partner in medical practice appear content with their family-work balance because the two have defined the basic assumptions of the practice to be congruent with their individual values and needs. The increasing numbers of women founding their own businesses indicate the widespread adoption of this independent approach to work among U.S. women.

The principals in The Pregnant Professor did not have the luxury of establishing their own organizational culture, however. Karen and Tim needed to find ways to adapt to work organizations that would be compatible with the needs of their marriage and their young child.

As the case makes clear, both individuals encountered specific and difficult underlying assumptions in their employing organizations that complicated their lives considerably. For example, Midwest University, at least in Karen's academic department, espoused values of long, isolated periods of work, with professional output of publications very rigidly prescribed. The basic assumptions of Karen's department, according to her subsequent mentor, even conflicted with some of the values and practices being used in other parts of the same organization. This highlights the importance that the assumptions of *one part* of an organization may have, even if in apparent contradiction with the procedures and espoused values of the organization as a whole.

Both Karen, at Worth College, and Tim, in his first faculty position in New York, found that the role of college teacher was more demanding and tiring than they had anticipated. Their socialization, in these two organizations, transmitted a set of values that required more work and energy than they previously realized. A variety of organizational procedures, particularly those related to the granting of tenure and pregnancy leave, embodied the underlying assumptions of the two educational institutions for which Karen worked. These procedures were important organizational artifacts in Karen's progress toward tenure and her personal desires for her family. It is clear that Midwest University subsequently responded to the needs of young professors in changing its tenure clock for professors adding children to their families. This change in artifact probably reflects a change in underlying assumptions as well.

The heavy demands of Tim's employing organizations, particularly in terms of hours on the job site and resumption of work immediately after the birth of his child, indicated that those organizations were still rather inflexible about the needs and schedules of young families. The situation faced by these two young professionals is precisely the concern of Friedan (1997) when she argues that fundamental workplace and economic restructuring are needed for the benefit of American families and communities. More recent analyses confirm the continuation of these high work expectations within the professions, with obvious impact of time for parenting and other family roles and responsibilities (Folby, 2001; Goldin, 2004; Hochschild, 1997). Our German case suggests that a complex interaction of public and private policies may further complicate family-friendly reforms in the workplace. While public leaders in Germany enacted policies to benefit families and children, these very policies sometimes reinforced traditional attitudes within businesses and other work organizations. Schein's (2004) analysis of the necessity of leadership commitment to the success of any proposed change in an organizational culture is firmly supported by the experiences of Carlotta and other German mothers. Changing one set of espoused values in the country, that is, attempting to promote gender-free advancement opportunities, when individual leaders in private organizations are not similarly engaged in promoting the change, has proven somewhat futile. In addition, attempting to encourage both a higher birthrate and the employment of women, within a surrounding culture conflicted about women's roles, has produced numerous dilemmas.

Of all the cases presented here, Sexual Harassment in the Military probably provides the most powerful illustration of the importance of organizational culture to gender issues and their improvement. The studies of harassment conducted by the military and the attention devoted to the issue by military leaders in the Army suggest that the espoused values of the military are definitely in opposition to the harassment described in the case. Yet the behavior has persisted. It is most likely that there are basic assumptions operating here—about the nature of effective military discipline and command, for example—that provide a protective cover for harassment, despite the attempts of leaders to stamp it out. Years of a male-dominated hierarchy, in which drill sergeants, senior cadets, and others in command are granted almost total authority, cannot be changed simply by espousing antiharassment values in official policy or even in well-designed training. Until vigorous leaders succeed in convincing military organizations that harassment is counterproductive and contrary to important basic values, the behavior is unlikely to be eliminated. In this regard, of course, the military is not unique; many contemporary organizations may reflect underlying assumptions that are tolerant of harassing behaviors.

If organizational culture is slow to change, then what are the respective roles of public policy and individual action in combating gender discrimination in the workplace? The actions of government are important in at least two ways. First, government policy models the desirable values about gender equity and treatment, whether or not all organizations are actually conforming to these values. Thus, the Glass Ceiling Commission charged the federal government with the obligation of being a model employer in eliminating the glass ceiling in government agencies. In Germany, the Alliance for Business, a government-sponsored initiative to promote family-friendly policies, may not have succeeded initially but may provide a framework for later progress (Vogelheim, 2005). This symbolic role of government is critical.

Second, government policy provides a basic framework of equity principles to which leaders in organizations and individual employees can appeal for remedy in a specific situation. It is important that Title VII exists; it provides the means of forcing organizations to at least change the artifacts of their culture—their formal procedures—to conform to the law. Of course, the law is only as effective as the willingness of individuals to appeal to it and the determination of government to enforce it. Many critics of equal employment law have effectively argued that lack of enforcement, for example, seriously weakens legal prohibitions against unequal pay, sexual harassment, and so on. In China, constitutional guarantees of gender equality do not seem universally implemented in the workplace. On the other hand, legal protection has undoubtedly assisted many courageous women, and their male supporters, to change the employment practices of many organizations in the past 30 years. (See, for example, Davis, 2005.)

This raises the importance of the *individual* in promoting workplace fairness and developing effective means of addressing gender issues at work. If individuals who need policy change or enforcement are unwilling to ask for it, then it will not occur. If leaders in organizations recognize that a practice is unfair or ineffective, they must on occasion be willing to directly confront the organizational culture on that issue. While individual actions, even those of leaders, do not necessarily "fix" an organization, they cumulatively raise awareness of gender issues and provide individual compensation in many instances for illegal or unfair treatment. The lawsuits filed by Meghan Evans and Kirsten Andersen confront the court with actual workplace practices and situations; in adjudicating these cases the courts eventually arrive at a consensus about standards by which to judge these matters and effective means of enforcement.

The case studies are messy. They do not resolve the gender issues neatly or in a universally popular fashion. The solutions to the problems presented are not clear and require not only careful analysis but also the acknowledgment that a variety of perspectives on the same situation may have merit. Thinking of the issues as global, which indeed they are, makes matters even more complex. If the cases have caused the reader to reflect on the nature of gender issues in the workplace and the multiple causes of these issues, as well as stimulated some creativity in possible approaches to the situations they present, then this short collection has succeeded.

❖ RELATED READINGS

Davis, M. F. (2005). Child care as a human right: A new perspective on an old debate. *Women, Politics & Policy, 21*(1–2), 173–180.

Folby, N. (2001). *The invisible heart: Economics and family values.* New York: New Press.

Friedan, B. (1963). *The feminine mystique.* New York: W. W. Norton.

Friedan, B. (1997). *Beyond gender: The new politics of work and family.* Baltimore, MD: Johns Hopkins University Press.

Garland, S. (1991, September 2). Commentary: How to keep women managers on the corporate ladder. *Business Week,* p. 64.

Goldin, C. (1990). *Understanding the gender gap: An economic history of American women.* New York: Oxford University Press.

Goldin, C. (2004, November). The long road to the fast track: Career and family. *Annals of the American Academy of Political and Social Science, 596,* 20–35.

Hochschild, A. R. (1997). *The time bind: When work becomes home and home becomes work.* New York: Metropolitan Books.

Jacobs, J. A., & Madden, J. F. (Eds.). (2004, November). Mommies and daddies on the fast track: Success of parents in demanding professions. [Special issue.] *Annals of the American Academy of Political and Social Science, 596.*

Jacobs, J. A., Madden, J. F., & Winslow, S. E. (2004). Overworked faculty: Job stresses and family demands. *Annals of the American Academy of Political and Social Science, 596,* 104–129.

Komaromy, M., Bindman, A. B., Haber, R. J., & Sande, M. A. (1993). Sexual harassment in medical training. *New England Journal of Medicine, 328,* 322–326.

Kuhn, T. (1970). *The structure of scientific revolutions.* Chicago: University of Chicago Press.

Schein, E. (2004). *Organizational culture and leadership* (3rd ed.). San Francisco: Jossey-Bass.

Vogelheim, E. (2005). The alliance for jobs in Germany: The promise and failure of gender mainstreaming. *Journal of Women, Politics & Policy, 21*(1–2), 163–172.

About the Author

Jacqueline DeLaat is McCoy Professor of Political Science at Marietta College in Ohio. She also teaches online for the University of Maryland's University College. In addition, she has lectured in China and Brazil, and in 2003 she was selected for a Fulbright Teaching Award. Her educational background is in U.S. politics and she holds a Ph.D. from the University of Pittsburgh in public administration. For more than twenty-five years she has taught political science in small liberal-arts institutions, with major teaching areas in public policy, public administration, U.S. politics and institutions, and women in politics and the workplace. She is known as an enthusiastic teacher, favoring active student projects and a dynamic classroom—including the frequent use of current event projects, case studies, and simulations.

Prior to her teaching career, she worked in the Washington, D.C., area and held a variety of administrative posts in government and in quasi-governmental organizations. Her Washington experience has enhanced both her subsequent teaching and her research. She has also consulted with several colleges and universities, as well as private and governmental organizations, on gender issues.

For the past decade, her professional agenda has focused on the development of teaching cases to prepare students and workers for gender issues in the contemporary workplace. Originally centered in the United States, the work has recently broadened to include case studies set in workplaces in other countries, including Brazil, China, and Germany. Her cases are frequently presented at international case study meetings and have won awards, including a special grant from the American Bar Association's Commission on Justice and Education. Within the political science community, she has presented on the pedagogy and development of case studies. In addition, she has presented at several international women's conferences and in 2005 conducted an interactive workshop on gender in the workplace at the first Women's Leadership Conference in Dubai, United Arab Emirates.